THE WISDOM OF ISRAEL REGARDIE

ಬಿ ಬಿ ಬಿ ಬಿ ಬಿ
Volume III
SELECTED ARTICLES, INTRODUCTIONS, PREFACES AND FOREWORDS

Introduction by
Lon Milo DuQuette

Some Other Titles From New Falcon Publications

Aha! The Sevenfold Mystery of the Ineffable Love
　　　　　　　　　　　　　　　　　　　　–Aleister Crowley
Bio-Etheric Healing　　　　　　　　　　–Trudy Lanitis
Undoing Yourself With Energized Meditation and Other Devices
Secrets of Western Tantra: The Sexuality of the Middle Path
Dogma Daze
　　　　　　　　　　　　　　–Christopher S. Hyatt, Ph.D.
Rebels & Devils; The Psychology of Liberation
　　　　　　　　　　–Edited by Christopher S. Hyatt, Ph.D.
Aleister Crowley's Illustrated Goetia
Taboo: Sex, Religion & Magick
Sex Magic, Tantra & Tarot: The Way of the Secret Lover
　　　　–Christopher S. Hyatt, Ph.D., and Lon Milo DuQuette
Pacts With The Devil
Urban Voodoo: A Beginner's Guide to Afro-Caribbean Magic
　　　　　　–Jason Black and Christopher S. Hyatt, Ph.D.
The Psychopath's Bible
　　　　　　–Christopher S. Hyatt, Ph.D., and Jack Willis
Ask Baba Lon　　　　　　　　　　–Lon Milo DuQuette
Aleister Crowley and the Treasure House of Images
　　　　　　　　　　　　　–J.F.C. Fuller, Aleister Crowley,
　　　　　　　Lon Milo DuQuette and Nancy Wasserman
Enochian World of Aleister Crowley
　　　　　　　–Lon Milo DuQuette and Aleister Crowley
Info-Psychology
Neuropolitique
The Game of Life
What Does WoMan Want?　　　　　–Timothy Leary, Ph.D.
Rebellion, Revolution and Religiousness　　　　　–Osho
Reichian Therapy: A PracticalGuide for Home Use
　　　　　　　　　　　　　　　　　　　　–Dr. Jack Willis
Woman's Orgasm: A Guide to Sexual Satisfaction
　　　　–Benjamin Graber, M.D., and Georgia Kline-Graber, R.N.
Shaping Formless Fire
Seizing Power
Taking Power　　　　　　　　　　　　–Stephen Mace
The Illuminati Conspiracy: The Sapiens System
　　　　　　　　　　　　　　　　　–Donald Holmes, M.D.
The Secret Inner Order Rituals of the Golden Dawn
　　　　　　　　　　　　　　　　　　　　　–Pat Zalewski
Sufism, Islam and Jungian Psychology
　　　　　　　　　　　　　　–J. Marvin Spiegelman, Ph.D.
Nonlocal Nature: The Eight Circuits of Consciousness
　　　　　　　　　　　　　　　　　–James A. Heffernan
on What is　　　　　　　　　　　　　　–Ja Wallin

Other Titles by Dr. Israel Regardie

A Garden of Pomegranates
A Practical Guide to Geomantic Divination - A Small Gem
Attract and Use Healing Energy - A Small Gem
Be Yourself - A Guide to Relaxation and Health
Ceremonial Magic
Dr. Israel Regardie's Definitive Work on Aleister Crowley,
  The Eye In The Triangle
Healing Energy, Prayer and Relaxation
How To Make and Use Talismans - A Small Gem
My Rosicrucian Adventure
Teachers of Fulfillment
The Art and Meaning of Magic - A Small Gem
The Body-Mind Connection, A Path to Well-Being - A Small Gem
The Complete Golden Dawn System of Magic
The Complete Golden Dawn System of Magic Book 1 - Ltd. Edition
The Complete Golden Dawn System of Magic Book 2 - Ltd. Edition
The Complete Golden Dawn System of Magic - The Black Edition
The Eye in the Triangle: An Interpretation of Aleister Crowley
The Golden Dawn Audio CDs, Vol. 1, Vol. 2, and Vol. 3
The Legend of Aleister Crowley
The Magic of Israel Regardie
The Middle Pillar
The Philosopher's Stone
The Portable Complete Golden Dawn System of Magic
The Tree of Life
The Wisdom of Israel Regardie - Vol. I
  Selected Introductions, Prefaces and Forewords
The Wisdom of Israel Regardie - Vol. II
  Selected Essays and Commentaries
The Wisdom of Israel Regardie - Vol. III
  Selected Articles, Introductions, Prefaces and Forewords
What You Should Know About the Golden Dawn
Aha! (Dr. Israel Regardie and Aleister Crowley)
Roll Away The Stone/The Herb Dangerous
    (Dr. Israel Regardie and Aleister Crowley)

MANY OF OUR TITLES AVAILABLE ON KINDLE!
Please visit our website at http://www.newfalcon.com

Copyright © 2020 New Falcon Publications

All rights reserved. No part of this book,
in part or in whole, may be reproduced, transmitted,
or utilized, in any form or by any means, electronic or mechanical,
including photocopying, recording, or by any information storage
and retrieval system, without permission in writing
from the publisher, except for brief quotations
in critical articles, books and reviews.

ISBN 13: 978-1-56184-562-0
ISBN 10: 1-56184-562-0

New Falcon Publications First Edition

The paper used in this publication meets the minimum requirements
of the American National Standard for Permanence of
Paper for Printed Library Materials Z39.48-1984

Printed in USA

NEW FALCON PUBLICATIONS
2046 Hillhurst Ave., Room 23
Los Angeles, CA 90027
www.newfalcon.com
email: info@newfalcon.com

THE WISDOM OF
ISRAEL REGARDIE

෴ ෴ ෴ ෴ ෴
Volume III
SELECTED ARTICLES, INTRODUCTIONS, PREFACES AND FOREWORDS

Introduction by
Lon Milo DuQuette

NEW FALCON PUBLICATIONS
Los Angeles, California

Introduction

Genius Can Be Infectious
By Lon Milo DuQuette

In my introductory words to the New Falcon Publications edition of *Dr. Israel Regardie's Definitive Work on Aleister Crowley - The Eye in the Triangle*[1] I confess:

> "No matter what you may have read to the contrary on the internet, I was not Regardie's 'magical apprentice.' Nor was I his formal student. I was never personally 'initiated' by him into any kind of Golden Dawn, or A∴A∴ or O.T.O.,[2] or anything. I can, however, proudly (and with no small measure of awe and humility) claim him as one of my earliest and most influential magical mentors. He made himself available whenever I had specific questions about magick and Crowley, and he was generous with his time, information and opinions. He was also supportive of our O.T.O. Lodge[3] in Newport Beach, and donated duplicate books from his own substantial library, and other magical trinkets."

Regardie initially gained the attention and admiration of the esoteric and occult community by his 1931 qabalistic primer, *A Garden of Pomegranates* which was almost immediately

---

[1] *Dr. Israel Regardie's Definitive Work on Aleister Crowley-The Eye in the Triangle*, New Falcon Publishing, First Edition 2017.

[2] We *were* both members of the Masonic youth organization, the Order of DeMolay, and upon discovery of this fact both stood up, and exchanged the Sign, Grip, and Secret Word of a DeMolay initiate.

[3] Heru-ra-ha Lodge Ordo Templi Orientis, chartered Jan.7th, 1978 by Hymenaeus Alpha 777 (Grady L. McMurtry). H.R.H. Lodge is the first local O.T.O. Lodge chartered under the auspices of the Grand Lodge of the United States, and remains the oldest continuously operating O.T.O. body in the world.

followed in 1932 by *The Tree of Life*. Both works are brilliant and deserving of occult immortality, but would soon be overshadowed by his controversial decision to publish (1937-1940) much of the (until then) "secret" magical teachings of the Hermetic *Order of the Golden Dawn* and its subsequent organizational incarnation, the *Stella Matutina*.

His credentials to write with insight and authority on such esoteric and arcane subjects were deservedly earned by his own scholarship, intelligence and brilliance, but his 'apprenticeship' (1928-1932) to Aleister Crowley would remain perhaps the most important item on his resume. If genius can said to be infectious it is easy to observe how it spread from Crowley to Regardie, and there is no question that their brief association knocked decades off young Regardie's learning curve. But I believe it also did something else.

Regardie lived and worked with Crowley during one of the most important and pivotal phases of Crowley's spiritual growth and development. Yes, Regardie was learning technical aspects of magick and esoteric philosophy, but more importantly he was experiencing firsthand the character-building effects (both positive and negative) that the illumination of a master has upon a student.

The two would eventually have a well-publicized falling-out, and Regardie would go on to make an honored and respectable name for himself. But, for better or worse, he would always remain somewhat in the shadow of the Great Beast, and in my opinion that is not necessarily a bad thing. I believe that because it is clear to me that to some degree *genius is infectious*.

I, for one, feel blessed to have had the opportunity to rub elbows with the genius of Israel Regardie, and am thrilled that his works, large and small are being made available to new generations.

Table of Contents

Introduction by *Lon Milo DuQuette*	vii

Selected Articles

Agape - The Occult Review Letter to R. G. Torrens, B.A.	3
The Complete Golden Dawn System of Magic Articles by Regardie as V.H. Frater Ad Majorem Adonai Gloriam	
The Enochian Language	13
An Addendum to the Book of Concourse	23
Discussion of The Z-Documents	57
Self-Initiation	71

Introductions

Aleister Crowley's *The World's Tragedy*	97
The Golden Dawn - An Account of the Teachings, Rites and Ceremonies of the Order of the Golden Dawn	
Introduction	105
The Complete Golden Dawn System of Magic by Regardie as V.H. Frater Ad Majorem Adonai Gloriam	
Introduction to the Magical Alphabet	177
777 and Other Qabalistic Writings of Aleister Crowley	
Including Gematria & Sepher Sephiroth	189

Prefaces and Forewords

Book 4 by Aleister Crowley, Preface to Parts 1 and 2	201
Magic Without Tears	203
The Alchemist's Handbook by Frater Albertus	225

SELECTED ARTICLES
by Israel Regardie

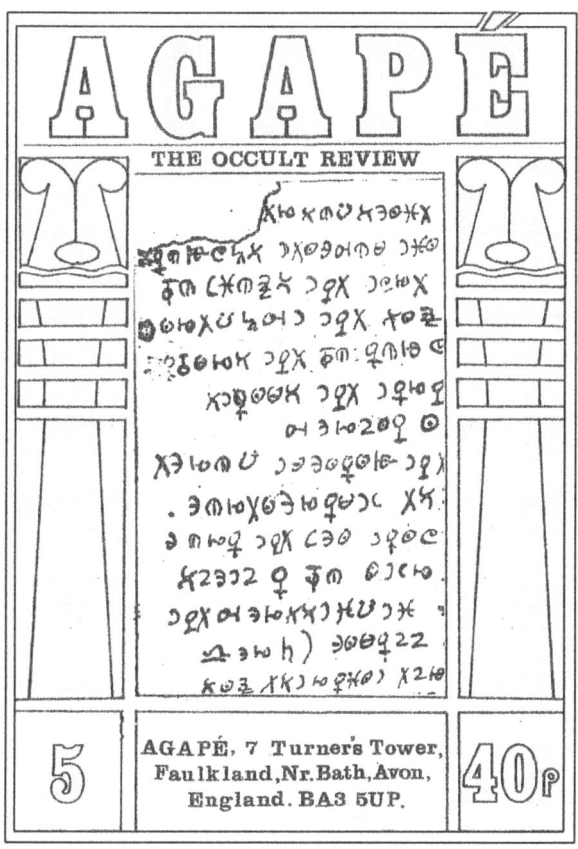

AGAPE - The Occult Review
Letter by Israel Regardie, 1969

MUCH ADO ABOUT NOTHING

The Golden Dawn's Inner teachings: R.G. Torrens, B.A. Neville Speareman, Long, 1969

The Secret Rituals of the Golden Dawn: R.G. Torrens, B.A. Aquarian Press, 1972, Northants.

Mr. R. G. Torrens, B.A. has recently authored the above named books. They are, by and large, monuments of fatuity and pompousness–and sometimes plain ignorance. In both these books he suffers from the delusion that the Crowley Tarot pack faithfully follows that of the Golden Dawn. It indicates that despite the thirty years he has spent in studying occult philosophy and special research into the techniques of the Golden Dawn, he has never seen the original Golden Dawn pack. This is no crime of course. On the other hand, it indicates that he has not taken the trouble to compare the descriptions of the Tarot cards in *Equinox 1. No. 8* (or in the 4th volume of my book *The Golden Dawn*) with those in *The Book Of Thoth* by Aleister Crowley. Had he done so, the enormous differences would have been apparent immediately.

Trump XXI in Crowley's handsome pack, is actually based on the Stele of Revealing; whereas the Golden Dawn card is not too dissimilar to that of Waite. The Fool in the Golden Dawn pack, depicts a young male child–a jester in motley is shown in the Crowley-Harris book. Finally, compare descriptions of the Ace of Wands in both packs. There are vast differences. Crowley's Tarot Pack, so aptly and beautifully painted by Lady Frieda Harris, is undoubtedly predicated on what he learnt in the Golden Dawn, but his spiritual experience of later years resulted in many vastly changed designs and meanings. The result is an entirely different Tarot pack.

Although my own Golden Dawn pack was stolen many years ago, I have enough data and some crude, minute photostat copies which should enable me to restore them. One of these days when leisure permits, I propose working with an artist to reproduce a full set of these Golden Dawn Tarot cards for publication. If and when that task is completed, I shall be happy to send R. G. Torrens, B.A., a complimentary pack, simply to let him know that he is far from knowing the facts despite his presumed "thirty years scholarship."

Incidentally, it is also apparent that he has not yet seen the Crowley pack itself, save as reproduced in *The Book Of Thoth*, published by Llewellyn Publications, Minneapolis. It has been available and for sale in the U.S. for a couple of years at least.

Another symptom of Mr. Torrens' asininity is his inclusion of the names of some members of Crowley's organisation in the same category of the Golden Dawn. His stated reason for this is the incorrect assumption that Crowley used rituals of initiation in his A∴A∴ and that these were those of the Golden Dawn. Nothing could be further from the truth than this!

I refer R.G. Torrens, B.A., to Crowley's essay *One Star in Sight*, for an extensive description of the structure of the A∴A∴ and the practical work connected with the grades, which nominally (only) are similar to those of the Golden Dawn. No one member knew any other member than the person introducing him to the Order and who then became his superior, and the person assigned to him at some later time as a personal student. Under these circumstances, no initiatory team could ever have been organised in the A∴A∴ to conduct such grade rituals. Mr. Torren's assumption is thus predicted on pure ignorance–and that is all–though that could have been easily obviated by some little reading of books noted in his bibliographies.

On page 202 of the second volume, Torrens quotes from *Equinox I, No. 8*, about ceremonial robes. This is actually an advertisement by William Notham, a tailor employed by Crowley to manufacture these robes. I must advise Mr. Torrens that there is simply no connection at all between these and those used in the Golden Dawn. It almost shows that, despite his frantic efforts at erudition, Mr. Torrens has no *practical* acquaintance with the Golden Dawn system. Had he made an attempt to *read–*

especially in his own work–the ritual descriptions of the gowns and cloaks used in the grade ceremonies, even he might have perceived the radical differences.

Another amusing evidence of his total lack of insight occurs on page 22 of the second book. He quotes from Liber *LXI vel Causae*, which is Crowley's historical account of the Golden Dawn and how and why the A∴A∴ was inaugurated. R.G. Torrens, B.A., states that it was written by a "brother of the A∴A∴ is none other than Crowley himself–a fact revealed often enough in the Equinox and elsewhere. Mr. Torrens' scholarship is not very careful or thorough.

Finally, let consideration be made of Mr. Torrens, B.A.'s, contention that his version of the initiatory grade rituals is so much more accurate and complete than those I published in *The Golden Dawn* in the thirties. First of all, let me assert unequivocally, that I never edited one word of the grade Rituals of the Order. They had already been revised when they came into my possession. However, I must confess that whoever did the revision did an excellent job of editing by eliminating much dead lumber and useless repetition. It is true that a couple of diagrams and their descriptions were deleted–these are restored in Mr. Torrens' *The Secret Rituals*–but I am compelled to admit that the salvation of my soul or advancement on the spiritual path will not be enhanced one iota by, for example, the inclusion of the diagram of the seven-branched candle stick or the table of shewbread.

If one compares the rituals in *The Golden Dawn* (Llewellyn Publications) with those in Mr. Torrens' book, one finds that in the opening of the rituals the numerous questions, asked by the Hierophant of the several officers, have been deleted. Instead, the officers–without being prompted by the Hierophant–simply state their nature, function and symbolism, in consecutive order. With the questions reinstated by Mr. Torrens, reading them merely constitutes a great expenditure of time and energy and is really a dreadful bore. This is even more true of the two grade rituals that Mr. Torrens does not give–The Portal and the Adeptus Minor rituals. Should Mr. Torrens, B.A., want me to believe that the inclusion of several such trivialities adds to the value and efficacy of the Ritual, I must conclude that he knows not whereof he speaks–as usual. I am reminded of the old aphorism: "empty vessels make a lot of noise."

This second volume is full of the most grotesque typographical errors. However, I may not judge him too harshly for this. However, I may not judge him too harshly for this. Proofreading is a burdensome chore–as I well know. Many of my own former book productions contain not a few similar instances of negligence and a "blind-eye".

His first volume I dealt with rather fully in the second edition of *My Rosicrucian Adventure* (Llewellyn Publications) which Mr. Torrens, B.A. has chosen to ignore. Ostriches do something of the same thing–I am given to understand. I was tempted to give a resume of that section here, to complete this review of Mr. Torrens' scholarship, but on second thoughts, it would be too tedious. Mr. Torrens B.A., is too easy to criticize–and his egotism, sticking out like a sore thumb, makes him far too vulnerable. I don't think anything would really be gained by so doing. Somewhere along the line, serious students will make their own comparisons between both of Mr. Torrens' books and *The Golden Dawn* (Llewellyn Publications) to discover for themselves the classical description of a windbag.

THE MAGICIANS OF THE GOLDEN DAWN, by ELLIC HOWE ROUTLEDGE & KEGAN PAUL, LONDON 1972. 3066pp. XIX foreword.

This book purports to be a documentary history of the Hermetic Order of the Golden Dawn. The foreword is by Gerald Yorke. Mr. Howe specifically claims to be a historian of underground movements, not an occultist or magician. Yorke on the other hand, was a disciple of Aleister Crowley over forty years ago; ordinarily he knows what he is talking about.

So far as the history is concerned, that matter can be disposed of quickly. It does admittedly reproduce some important letters and other fascinating documents relating to the early days of the Order, together with some juicy morsels of scandal of one kind and another; but that's as far as it goes. Howe indulges so liberally in sneers, guesses, inferences, suppositions, sarcasms, assumptions etc., as to wholly invalidate its claim to be a history. There is no real proof or tangible evidence of Howe's major contention–merely guesswork.

His thesis is that after Mm. Blavatsky founded the Theosophical Society in 1875 to disseminate the Eastern Wisdom Religion under orders from her masters, Dr. William Wynn Westcott, a high grade mason, decided to go her one better. He is alleged to have forged documents to prove he was under authority from "Secret Chiefs" to form an Order to teach the Western Magical Tradition. Still unaccounted for are the cypher manuscripts, upon which the whole mystery is still based. A good case is ALMOST made, but since a miss is as good as a mile. Howe's as assumptions, guesses and inferences are totally worthless. And this despite his recourse to graphologists and other authorities.

One of the virtues of the book is the usual expose of human foibles and weaknesses with which we are all familiar but which somehow seem to be brilliantly spotlighted in an occult milieu. The list of members provided by the author is indeed impressive. Indeed, many of them were brilliant people, but all the evidence presented does less to show that the Golden Dawn was a hoax as to prove that human nature is a pretty flimsy combination of diverse characteristics and traits. The ridiculous search for Masters, which seems to be with us always, also harangued the Order in those days. The book also demonstrates how far the members wandered from the true aims of the Order as expressed and developed in the various obligations and oaths. Many of them seemed to wobble all over the place except in the direction suggested by the Adeptus Minor obligation. If the book does no more than to demonstrate these facts, it could still be a useful and successful book, provided that the readers who are prone to go hunting for Masters and do all the silly things some of the Golden Dawn members did take this very seriously to heart. However, I doubt they will even see it.

It is only in Yorke's critique. I assert unequivocally that Yorke's critique. I assert unequivocally that Yorke's damning foreword is wholly without basis, being rooted solely in his misunderstanding or lack of direct knowledge of Golden Dawn teaching.

For example: two pages are given over to a description of the Golden Dawn temple equipment. This description, however, is extrapolated practically verbatim from *Part II of Book Four* by Aleister Crowley. It is NOT Golden Dawn teaching.

Where is Yorke's discrimination?

There IS a vast difference, even though Crowley is in direct line of descent from the Golden Dawn. In the Neophyte ritual there is an obligation which, so Yorke says, omits any reference to the purpose to which the powers resulting from successful, practice of magic should be put. Nonsense! I refer Yorke to page 37 Vol. II, *The Golden Dawn* (Llewellyn Publications), to the cautionary address of the Hierophant to the newly inducted Neophyte. I further direct Yorke's attention to the paper: "On The General Guidance and Purification of the Soul" given to every Neophyte (p. 146, Vol. I *Golden Dawn*). Both disprove his contention.

So far as concerns the Adeptus Minor Obligation, it does admittedly bind the candidate to "purify and exalt my spiritual nature so that with the Divine Aid I may attain to be more than human and...unite myself to my higher and Divine Genius". Yorke's apprehension is that the student may soon imagine that, being more than human, he is God, instead of remaining as servant of God. Let me remind Yorke that on page 214-5, Vol. I, *Golden Dawn* ("On the Microcosm"), it is clearly stated that the higher Genius is but an Angel on one of the lowest hierarchical rungs, as it were, of a vast spiritual ladder, beyond which are mighty archangelic and Divine forces. This should be enough to humble anyone who can read, save the most arrogant and egotistic idiot–the likes of which may be found in any religion or Order, in the East or in the West.

That Mathers, who at first assisted Westcott in the formation of the Order, became arrogant, pompous and dictatorial is self evident. But he needs no defence; he was only human, and like many of us, "fell from grace". At the same time, this history proves that IF he wrote the Adeptus Minor Ritual by himself (which I seriously doubt), and if he did elaborate the crude Dee-Kelly system into that elaborate Enochian system which is the crown of the Order itself, then he was an undisputed spiritual genius of the highest magnitude. What is now required is a history of this most extraordinary man. S. L. McGregor Mathers who became the head of the Golden Dawn, was no ordinary person, whatever his obvious character defects may have been.

If Mathers got the Golden Dawn teachings from books in the British Museum, so insinuates Ellic Howe, I ask for references to such simple matters as the Pentagram Ritual, skrying in the Spirit Vision, Telesmatic images, the Assumption of Godforms and many other teachings of the Order. I assure Howe that he won't find them there, I myself have spent many months looking for similar origins in the same place amongst the Sloane and Harlem manuscripts. Admittedly much material was borrowed from books he consulted in the British Museum. Any idiot could have done that. But to integrate that mass of traditional material into a systematic whole, tied together with previously unknown data and techniques, is a horse of a different color.

I also assure both Howe and Yorke that no part of the so-called Bornless Ritual, of which Yorke is most critical as resulting in an inflated ego, was ever used in any OFFICIAL Golden Dawn ritual. If any individual member, including Mathers, did make private use of it, that's another ballgame in a different field.

And when will these scholars realise that the literal translation from this early ritual fragment as "headless" does not mean without a head, but simply without a beginning–eternal or Bornless. *Rosh ha-shanah* in Hebrew does not mean the Head of the Year, but the New or Beginning of the Year. It is idiomatic only. Let's keep it that way; it requires no derision.

Yorke winds up his Foreword with a reference to Aleister Crowley, our one-time guru of forty years ago. The Golden Dawn had given birth to its first pseudo-Messiah. No more need be said".

While holding no brief for Crowley, a real crumb on the level of inter-personal relationships, I can only hope both Yorke and I will be around on this planet for another decade or so. I think Crowley has still a couple of tricks up his sleeve, and we may be startled by the prophecy dictated to him nearly seventy years ago, in the BOOK OF THE LAW relative to: I am the warrior Lord of the Forties; the Eighties cower before me, & are abased." The impact of the cosmic forces to be released about then. We shall then see how phoney he was if we but remember that the world in which he lived was a quiet, placid and peaceful one.

Hoax? Fiddlesticks!

ISRAEL REGARDIE

The Complete Golden Dawn System of Magic
Articles by Israel Regardie
as V.H. Frater Ad Majorem Adonai Gloriam
Copyright 1984-2020

THE ENOCHIAN LANGUAGE

Our earliest knowledge of this alphabet and language is derived from the skrying of Sir Edward Kelley and Dr. John Dee towards the end of the sixteenth century. This was in the time both of Mary Queen of Scots and Queen Elizabeth the First of England. In point of fact, Dr. John Dee became Queen Elizabeth's friend, astrologer and confidante. According to some of the latest research, Dr. John Dee was not the gullible, credulous spiritualist as some critics have alleged, but was in fact a true man of the Renaissance–a competent scientist, geographer and interestingly enough, a secret agent under the tutelage of Sir Francis Walsingham.

This alphabet and language is called Angelic or Enochian, as the Angels who instructed both Dee and Kelley claimed to be those who had once conversed with the patriarch Enoch of the Bible. Kelley was the skryer and used a shewstone or crystal ball, which is now in the British Museum. In this ball he saw Angels who instructed him to make large charts and designs which Dr. Dee would have before him on a desk, while Kelley was skrying. When an Angel in the shewstone would point to a certain letter on one of his charts, Kelley, in his turn, would pass the information on to Dr. Dee as for example: Table B, Column 7, Rank 11, etc. Dr. Dee would locate the letter and write it down, awaiting the next.

This was a slow and tedious method of gaining information. All of these conversations and instructions were recorded by Dr. Dee in diaries, still to be found in the British Museum in the Sloane and Harleian collection of manuscripts. In the year 1659, Meric Casaubon published a large tome reproducing the details of some of these conversations and instructions. In this book are to be found dozens of prayers offered humbly by Dee that he be guided in the right direction; many are beautiful, others are long and tedious.

From this basic material has grown one of the most complete systems of magical endeavor that was ever so beautifully and systematically organized, beyond even the wildest dreams of Dee and Kelley, by the Hermetic Order of the Golden Dawn towards the end of the nineteenth century.

As can be seen when consulting Meric Casaubon, many of the invocations–or Calls as they are named, dictated by the Angels, were given in reverse. It was felt that the Enochian words were so powerful that direct dictation would call forth powers and forces not then desired. The present dictionary in this Volume of the Enochian language has been compiled from words used in the nineteen invocations that were given to Dee and Kelley. Over a period of time, it has become possible to separate the prefixes and suffixes from the basic Enochian words. Since I am no philologist this was no easy task, especially as it was soon recognized that in the process of repeated copyings, by uninformed members of the Golden Dawn, many errors had crept into the text. Words in one invocation had to be checked against similar words in another invocation to arrive at some semblance of accuracy. Recently the words in this dictionary have been checked against those found in Casaubon's enormous tome. Even here, a fantastic number of errors were perceived and I became aware of what a momentous task it had been to compile this dictionary in the mid-thirties.

Though ordinarily I have assiduously avoided self-praise, I must confess, as I examine this dictionary after a time interval of nearly fifty years, that as simple dictionaries go, this is not such a bad job after all. The separation of the suffixes and prefixes from the proper root words was, in itself, no mean accomplishment, especially when one considers that no clue is to be found either in the Golden Dawn documents or in Crowley's renditions of the Calls in *Equinox I, #8*. Languages are not amongst my few accomplishments. My English is good, my French is execrable (as the maitre d' of a French restaurant I used to frequent can testify), I know but little Latin and Greek. So far as Hebrew is concerned, though I did study that intensively years ago, with the intent of translating some old Qabalistic texts, that project vanished into thin air before my second decade was out.

The Enochian language is not just a haphazard combination and compilation of divine and angelic names drawn from the Tablets. Apparently, it is a true language with a grammar and syntax of its own. Only a superficial study of the invocations suffice to indicate this to be a fact. The invocations are not strings of words and barbarous names, but are sentences which can be translated in a meaningful way and not merely transliterated.

The Enochian language is without any history prior to the skrying of Edward Kelley and John Dee. There is no record of its prior existence, regardless of some fanciful theories which have been invented to account for it. Many present-day philologists have often pointed out that it is impossible for any single human being to invent a language of his own, complete with errors, such as we find in the transcribing in Dr. Dee's diaries. Any inventor today would be careful enough to be more thorough in the construction of his language than were Dee and Kelley, or the Angels who originally dictated the Calls.

The Enochian alphabet consists of twenty-one letters which can be transposed into English. The individual letters are known to us in both the printed or elaborate style and also in a script or cursive form.

One of the curious anomalies about this Enochian alphabet is that each letter has a name, as in other languages, such as in Greek: Alpha, Beta, Gamma, etc., but this Enochian name bears absolutely no relationship to the **sound** value of the letter itself. Alpha in Greek is given the sound value of A; in Hebrew Gimel is given the sound value of G, etc.: but in Enochian, Veh, has the sound value of C or K, not of V, as one might at first have supposed.

Since the names of the letters are not commonly used, the use of the English alphabetical order and pronunciation is recommended in order to avoid the elaborate and cursive style and also in the given us by tradition. In passing, I should not that the cursive style is used but rarely, and for that reason is not worth committing to memory.

In the original Golden Dawn papers written by MacGregor Mathers and William Wynn Westcott, certain rules were laid down for the pronunciation of the Enochian words. Mathers advised that the consonants should be followed by the vowel which obtains in the corresponding Hebrew letters. For example: the word "sobha" could be pronounced soh-bay-hah. The god-names, like MPH ARSL GAIOL, to be found in the Water Tablet, are pronounced as: Em-pay-hay Ar-sel Gah-ee-Ohl. The one major exception to all rules is that the letter Z is **always** pronounced as zoad. So that the word Zamran is pronounced as Zoad-ah-mer-ah-noo.

Dr. Westcott laid down similar rules in another document he wrote for the Adeptus Minor, but his version gives several variations which should be noted. I have found these latter to be valid, making for greater euphony and ease in handling. He said: "M is pronounced em; N is pronounced en (also Nu or Noo–since in Hebrew the vowel following the equivalent letter Nun is used); A is pronounced ah; P is peh; S is ess; D is deh." This rule, in fact, simplifies the entire procedure. If one had no further rules than these, the entire matter of Enochian pronunciation, which has been unnecessarily obscured and rendered so difficult, could then be handled with ease.

Another variation is that Y, J and I are similar to the Yod in Hebrew–as U and V are similar to the Vau in Hebrew. X has sometimes the value of Samekh and at others of Tzaddi, though there is no reason not to use it as in English.

Usage and experience will ultimately dictate which one is to be employed. Let me give several examples of words chosen relatively at random in order to exemplify the simplicity of the process of pronunciation. These names are to be found in the Tablet of Union:

EXARP	**Ex-ar-pay**
HCOMA	**Hay-coh-mah**
NANTA	**En-ah-en-tah**
BITOM	**Bay-ee-toh-em**

Though it has been suggested by Westcott that *every* letter should be pronounced separately, this idea makes for clumsiness, lack of euphony and unnecessary length, which creates fatigues and monotony. Further examples are:

CHIS	**Cah-hee-sah**
CHISGE	**Cah-his-jee**

The student must use not merely these rules but his own sense of euphony and intuition in dealing with this matter. Remember, there is no final version which is absolutely authoritative.

In the Portal grade of *The Complete Golden Dawn System of Magic* (Falcon Press, Phoenix 1983) there is a very short Enochian invocation which is abbreviated from the First Call, but also contains the names of three Archangels drawn from the Tablet of Union. I give the invocation first, followed by its transliteration in pronounceable phrases.

> "OL SONUF VAORSAGI GOHO IADA BALTA, LEXARPH, COMANAN, TABITOM. ZODAKARA EKA ZODAKARE OD ZODAMARAN. ODO KIKLE QAA, PIAPE PIAMOEL OD VAOAN."

This means, "I will reign over you, saith the God of Justice. Lexarph, Comanan, Tabitom. Move therefore. Show yourselves forth and appear. Declare unto us the mysteries of your creation, the balance of righteousness and truth."

The pronunciation of these few lines of Enochian language is nowhere near as formidable as may appear at first sight. The following is the pronunciation I use. I might add in passing that this is an Invocation I have used frequently over the last forty-odd years, primarily in relationship to the practice of the Middle Pillar technique (which I have improved and enhanced, to be published by Falcon Press under the title *The Sceptre of Power*) and the Ritual of the "Watch Tower Ceremony" in this volume.

> "Oh-el Soh-noof Vay-oh-air-sah-jee, Goho Ee-ah-dah Baltah. El-ex-arpay-hay. Cohmah-nah-noo. Tah-bee-toh-em. Zoad-a-kay-rah ay-kah zoad-a-kay-ray oh-dah Zoad-a-mer-ah-noo. Oh-dah kee-klay kah-ah. Pee-ah-pay pee-ah-moh-el oh-dah vay-of-ah-noo."

Using these as an example, the enterprising student should experience very little difficulty in handling any words or phrases to be found in the various Calls or in this dictionary. The major obstacle at first encountered is simply the strangeness of the appearance of the words and the lack of experience in pursuing the rules laid down. The sounds may seem very much like pure gibberish at the outset. If he persists, however, the student will soon learn to disentangle the sounds from apparent chaos and find himself confronted by a meaningful language and a meaningful set of invocations. In any event, do remember there is no absolute or final rendition of the way to pronounce these Calls. If he can approximate the instructions lad down here, his own version will be as authoritative as any.

In 1976, an Enochian Dictionary was published by Leo Vinci entitled **GMICALZOMA** through the Regency Press in England. I have no comments to make about it, other than that it is a workable and usable dictionary. It post-dates my Dictionary by many years, mine having begun to circulate in the U.S. and the United Kingdom a score of years earlier.

Not too long after that, Askin Publishers in England became interested in my dictionary and a correspondence ensued relative to having them publish mine. A friend, a philologist, promised to write an Introduction to it with a view to elucidating the origins of the Enochian language. Again, a series of mishaps occurred which prevented the Introduction from being written. It resulted in Askin Publishers taking the lead, and offering to get Dr. Laycock (an Australian philologist who had been in touch with me sometimes before this) to do an Introduction for it. When the Introduction arrived, I was most disappointed in it, feeling that it exuded contempt and ridicule.

My next step was to telephone Askin Publishers in London to confess my total disappointment and stating that if they insisted on publishing Laycock's Introduction with my Dictionary, I would withdraw the latter. So it came to pass that Askin Publishers returned my Dictionary at my request. Sometime in the next immediate period they must have formulated a Dictionary which they published with the Laycock Introduction.

These facts need to be mentioned solely to establish the priority of my Dictionary. Not that it matters very much. There was a need for this Dictionary amongst students of Magic, and someone got there first.

The history of the Enochian Dictionary that is being published here should not be without interest.

Shortly after having been elevated to the Adeptus Minor Grade, I began an intensive study of the Enochian system, including the beginning of a Dictionary. The study of the system resulted in my writing a paper entitled *An Addendum to the Book of Concourse of Forces*, included in this volume. Within a couple of years, the Dictionary had achieved a well-defined form–that is by 1940-41. Then World War II intervened, when it was put aside with a number of other similar projects until the 1950s. During that time, the Dictionary was loaned to a number of different people on both sides of the Atlantic. Ordinarily I would not use names, but in this instance I feel it is incumbent upon me to do so.

There was a young man in Surrey, a protege of an osteopathic friend of mine A.E. Charles, to whom I lent it early in the 1950s–altogether apart from a handful of students here in the U.S. Somewhere around 1956, I was visited in Los Angeles by Miss Tamara Bourkoun, a very ardent and knowledgeable student of Co-Masonry and the occult. Amongst other things, including the *Golden Dawn Tarot Deck*, I loaned her the *Enochian Dictionary* with my permission to copy it for her use if she so willed. From then on, it had some kind of circulation here and there among the more serious students of Magic who took the Enochian system seriously.

Early in the 1970s **Sangreal Foundation**, who had already published several of my things, were toying with the idea of seeing that the *Enochian Dictionary* was finally published. However again some unforeseen events occurred which precluded the possibility of that happening.

Now under the direction of the **Israel Regardie Foundation** and Falcon Press, this long awaited work has found itself in print, in this particular volume.

AN ADDENDUM TO THE BOOK OF THE CONCOURSE OF THE FORCES POSTSCRIPT TO ENOCHIANA

(This thesis was written in 1935 following an intensive study of the Golden Dawn documents on the Enochian system. It has been left virtually in the same form it had at that time.)

That the Enochian scheme is a vast and extensive one is well known to the Zelator Adeptus Minor. But that it is as extensive as actually it is, is suspected I am sure by few. For the complete system of the Enochian Tablets comprises, in reality, several apparently disconnected schemes–most of which are not even known to the average Z.A.M. Though they are unknown is not to say that they are unimportant, for it requires but little perspicacity to realize that the Enochian system underlies a large part of the important work of the Order.

There are many hints to indicate that the Z.A.M. is not in full possession of all the Enochian knowledge. As the Adeptus Minor ritual so eloquently observes of but one of the parts of the system: "Before the Door of the Tomb, as symbolic Guardians, are the Elemental Tablets and the Kerubic Emblems, even as before the mystical Gate of Eden stood the watchful Kerubim and the Sword of Flame. Do not therefore forget that the Tablets and the Kerubim are the Guardians of the Tomb of the Adept…"

The whole system comprises the following segments:

1. Liber Enoch - (Liber Logaeth), these are the Enochian Tablets.
2. The Claves Angelicae.
3. Liber Scientiae Auxiliis et Victoriae Terrestris.
4. Sigllum Dei Aemeth.
5. Heptarchia Mystica.
6. The Round Tablet of Nalvage.

The first two items above have been dealth with very adequately in the routine instructions provided for the Zelator Adeptus Minor in such documents as The Book of the Concourse of the Forces, as well as in the various introductions and digests made of that book, and also in the Ritual "T" known as The Book of the Forty Eight Angelical Keys or Calls.

The remaining schemes are not dealt with at all the study programme of work prescribed for the Z.A.M. In various places of those manuscripts there are deliberate gaps, indicating that such and such an item of knowledge does not come within the sphere of knowledge of the Z.A.M.

Nonetheless a certain amount of light can be thrown without too much difficulty upon these deliberate gaps, though whether or not they will be considered important depends wholly on how much of the ordinary Enochian material already available has been assimilated and appreciated by the Z.A.M.

Although in this paper I propose to concern myself almost exclusively with the third of the foregoing schemes, to show its relation to the previous two which are summarized in the material freely circulated within the Order, a few words in description of the others may be found useful.

The Sigillum Dei Aemeth consists of a highly elaborate Pentacle, said to be a magical synthesis of ideas of a purely spiritual nature with regard to Divine, Archangelic and Angelic Names concerned with the celestial spheres wherein operate the planetary forces. The latter are but the palaces or thrones of the forces depicted by the Sigillum. That this is so may be gathered from a statement uttered by the Angel MICHAEL in his communications to the skryers–Dr. John Dee and Sir Edward Kelley–who were responsible for the recording of this system:

"When thou wilt have anything to do in the world, in human affairs, seek nothing in Sigillo Aemeth. Enoch, his book, is a worldly book. Veritas in Coelo, Imago veritatis, in herra homini, Imago imagini respondet. Coelestia autem petuntur a Coelo."

In Ritual "T," it is mentioned that Irwin's manuscript gave certain names after the first 18 Keys. Most of these names appear on the enclosed Heptagrams of the Sigillum.

(The Order documents do not explain who this mysterious Irwin is, though his name is used several times. However, Waite in his Brotherhood of the Rosy Cross refers to him and clears up the mystery, though in his usual sarcastic way it seems as if he had no use for Major Irwin.)

Moreover, it must be noted that the Sigils attributed to the four Enochian Tablets–a Cross, a Sun with 12 Rays, and a Cross in whose angles are b4, 6b and a (T) with 4 Yods above it, receive their elucidation from this Sigillum, being resolved into the names of so-called Four Great Overseer-Angels of these Tablets.

The Heptarchia Mystica is very closely related to the former system, for it gives the names and sigils and invocations of the Angels and the lesser Spirits of the Planets. It touches a much lower plane than the Sigillum, the heavens of Assiah as it were, while the Sigillum soars to the worlds of Briah and Yetzirah. The world of Atziluth is touched through the system of Liber Scientiae Auxiliis et Victoriae Terrestris. Moreover, the Heptarchical Mystery gives an additional seven Tablets which are rather different in content and structure from the four Elemental Tablets we know already.

The schemes numbers 1-5 are very intimately related to the Enochian system and one to another. Item 6, the Round Table of Nalvage, however, is a magical Tablet which for the moment I have been unable to relate to the others. The communicating Angel NALVAGE dictated, in much the same way as did Ave and Michael in other connections, a series of letters and words which were to be arranged in a certain manner. They begin ZIR MOZ IAD—Zodireh Mozod Iada–"I am the Joy of God." etc. What the practical application of this Tablet is remains yet to be discovered. It consists of four very small Tablets, each of nine letters, in all of which IAD figures in four distinct permutations, surrounded by four words of five letters each, making 32 letters. Whether this fact connects it with the four Terrestrial Tablets and the Tablet of Union I can hardly say at this time. Of this Tablet, NALVAGE stated: "The substance is God the Father. The circumference is God the Son. The order and knitting together is God the Holy Ghost." etc. This does suggest the three columns or the cross bar and double Pillars of the Central Cross of the Tablets–Linea Spiritus Sancti, Linea Dei Patris Filiique.

To refer back to Liber Scientae Auxiliis, as a preliminary point, let it be noted that in Ritual "T," the following passages occur: "The application of the Keys of the 30 Aethrys does not come into the knowledge of the Z.A.M. Now although these Keys are thus to be employed to aid thee in the Skrying of the Tablets in the Spirit Vision, and in magical working therewith, yet shalt though know that they be allotted unto a much higher plane than the operation of the Tablets in the Assiatic World. And therefore are they thus employed in bringing the Higher Light and the

All-potent Forces into action herein. And so also, they are not to be profaned, or used lightly with an impure or frivolous mind."

In other words, it relates to the schema described in the Order manuscript entitled The Microcosm which lays down the philosophical dictum that the Kether of Man, "his Yechidah is his Divine Consciousness because it is the only part of man which we can touch the All-potent Forces. Behind Yechidah are the Angelic and Archangelic Forces of which the Yechidah is the manifestor. It is therefore the lower Genius or Viceroy of the Higher Genius which is beyond, and which is an Angel Mighty and Terrible. This Great Angel is the Higher Genius, beyond which are the Archangelic and Divine."

What is to be observed from this is, that of the same nature as the Higher Genius are the all-potent macrocosmic forces called forth by the Keys of the Aethyrs, as shown by the fact that though 91 in number, which equals AMN, the latter has a gematria of 741 which reduces to 12. And 12 is the gematria of HUA, the great Avenging Angel, the holy and divine Genius in KETHER. And the invocation of these forces is to be undertaken in fulfillment of the Obligation wherein in the 5-6 initiate swore on the Cross to apply himself to the Great Work so that, one day, he might become more than human, etc. Thus no frivolous is ignorant mind could invoke these divine forces without bringing serious spiritual and physical harm to himself, as the Ritual "T" duly and rightly warns.

The second point to be notices is that to construct the Enochian Tablets entirely with capital letters is a serious mistake. It may be useful to do so for the sake of convenience or of increased legibility. But so doing obscures one of the several important functions of the Tablet. Certain letters thereon should appear in lower case letters and other in capitals. It is from these latter capital letters that are constructed the names of mighty Angelical Princes who rule in each of the thirty Aethyrs. To each of the Aethyrs there are attributed three Governors or Angelical Princes, with the exception of the thirtieth Aethyr names TEX, in which there are four.

Thus, the Tablets enshrine, in addition to those names already described by The Book of the Concourse of the Forces, the names of Ninety One Angelical Princes whose rule is in the Thirty Aethyrs of the Macrocosmic World.

91 equals the Gematria of Aleph Mem Nun which equals Amen, as mentioned previously. And Amen equals Amoun, the concealed One, the Opener of the Day. Hence also are the names of these 91 Princes opened up and yet concealed in all secrecy in the Four Terrestrial Tablets and the Mystical Tablet of Union. Note that Amoun is concealed within the heart of the God-Man YSHhVH (whose Gematria is 326.) 91 + 326 equals 417 equals 12. And twelve is the Gematria of the great Angel HUA.

The scheme delineated at length in the book Liber Scientiae Auxiliis et Victoriae Terrestris, further conceives that each of these Angelic Princes is under the governancy of some one of the mighty Archangels ruling the mystical twelve Tribes of Israel together with the twelve Signs of the Zodiac. They are given in a special order which corresponds to the order of the Archangels depicted in the Zelator diagram of the Shewbread. There is, nevertheless, a slight discrepancy in the order of the Names of the Tribes are related to the Archangels. Rectified, the attribution may be noted as below:

Aries
The Tribe is Gad, the Diety name AOZPI, the Archangelic name is MALCHIDAEL and the Governing Angelic name is OLPAGED.
Taurus
The Tribe is Ephraim, the Diety name MOR, the Archangelic name is ASMODEL and the Governing Angelic name is ZIRACAH.
Gemini
The Tribe is Manasseh, the Deity name is DIAL, the Archangelic name is AMBRIEL and the Governing Angelic name is HONONOL.
Cancer
The Tribe is Issachar, the Deity name HCTGA, the Archangelic name is MURIEL and the Governing Angelic name is ZARNAAH.
Leo
The Tribe is Judah, the Deity name is OIP, the Archangelic name is VERCHIEL and the Governing Angelic name is GEBABAL.
Virgo
The Tribe is Naphthali, the Deity name is TEAA, the Archangelic name is HAMALIEL and the Governing Angelic name is ZURCHOL.
Libra
The Tribe is Asshur, the Deity name is PDOCE, the Archangelic name is ZURIEL and the Governing Angelic name is ALPUDUS.
Scorpio
The Tribe is Dan, the Deity name MPH, the Archangelic name is BARACHIEL and the Governing Angelic name is CADAAMP.
Sagittarius
The Tribe is Benjamin, the Deity name ARSL, the Archangelic name is ADVACHIEL and the Governing Angelic name is ZARZILG.

Capricorn

The Tribe is Zebulun, the Deity name GAIOL, the Archangelic name is HANAEL and the Governing Angelic name is LAVAVOTH.

Aquarius

The Tribe is Reuben, the Deity name ORO, the Archangelic name is CAMBRIEL and the Governing Angelic name is ZINGGEN.

Pisces

The Tribe is Simeon, the Deity name IBAH, the Archangelic name is AMNITZIEL and the Governing Angelic name is ARFAOLG.

In classifying these names I have arranged the appropriate Great and Secret Holy Names of God as they appear on the Elemental Tablets following the suggestion made in S.A.'s Ritual where this passage occurs:

"Apply this scheme to the Earth treating the Three Deity Names as the Three Signs of the Zodiac in one quarter. Thus, take the Fire Tablet and place OIP in Leo, TEAA in Virgo, PDOCE in Libra, and so on with the other God-names, treating the Kerubic signs as the "point-de-depart"; one quarter of a House in Astrology will also be roughly equal to the square of each letter."

The above classification provides a comprehensive scheme to be used by itself, alone, or in collaboration with the Angelic Names of the Schem-hamphoresch, of great value in the art of invocation. In invocation, the two sets of names could be used conjointly to generate a good deal of power. The Pentagram could be used with the Archangelic name, together with the appropriate permutations of Tetragrammaton, as indicated by the Sepher Yetzirah. The

Governing Angelic Name could be used in the Hexagram, using the appropriate figure of the planet ruling the Sign–Mars for Aries, and Jupiter for Pisces, etc., using not the Sigil of the planet but the Sigil of the Zodiacal Sign.

The tabulation of the Names which now follow provides the names of:

The Aire or Aethyr itself.
The Name of the Angelical Governor of the Division.
The Number of the Tribes of Israel and its Presiding Archangel.
The Number of ministers and attendants.

Before proceeding to this classification, the Z.A.M. may recall that in Ritual "T" the following passage occurs: "The Numbers 456 and 6739 etc., which occur in some of the Calls contain Mysteries will be found to be self-explanatory by referring to the final column of the following Table which classifies in systematic order the Aethyrs, their Governors and their Angels, together with the number of subservient attendants.

1st LIL
OCCODON Ninth, 7209, PASCOMB Eleventh, 2360, VALGARS Seventh, 5562.
2nd ARN
DOAGNIS Fourth, 3636, PACASNA Second, 2362, DIALIVA Second, 8962.
3rd ZOM
SAMAPHA Ninth, 4400, VIROOLI Seventh, 3660, ANDISPI Tenth, 9236.
4th PAZ
THOTANF Tenth, 2360, AXZIARG Tenth, 3000, POTHNIR Twelfth, 6300.

5th LIT
   LAZDIXI First, 8630, NOCAMAL Seventh, 2306, TIARPAX Eleventh, 5802.
6th MAZ
   SAXTOMP Fifth, 3620, VAVAAMP Twelfth, 9200, ZIRZIRD Fifth, 7220.
7th DEO
   OBMACAS Fourth, 6363, GENADOL Third, 7706, ASPIAON Eleventh, 6320.
8th ZID
   ZAMFRES Fifth, 4362, TODNAON First, 7236, PRISTAC Ninth, 2302.
9th ZIP
   ODDIORG Third, 9996, CRALPIR Tenth, 3620 DOANZIN Ninth, 4230.
10th ZAX
   LEXARPH Eleventh, 8880, COMANAN Seventh, 1230, TABITOM Ninth, 1617.
11th ICH
   MOLPAND Tenth, 3472, VANARDA Sixth, 7236, PONODOL Third, 5234.
12th LOE
   TAPAMAL Sixth, 2658, GEDOONS Eighth, 7772, AMBRIAL Second, 3391.
13th ZIM
   GECAOND Tenth, 8111, LAPARIN First, 3360, DOCEPAX Seventh, 4213.
14th VTA
   TEDOOND Fifth, 2673, VIVIPOS Seventh, 9236, OOANAMB Twelfth, 8230.

15th OXO
TAHANDO Ninth, 1367, NOCIABI Tenth, 1367, TASTOXO Twelfth, 1886.

16th LEA
COCARPT Second, 9920, LANACON Third, 9230, SOCHIAL Twelfth, 9240.

17th TAN
SIGMORF Second, 7623, AYDROPT Fifth, 7132, TOCARZI Ninth, 2634.

18th ZEN
NABAOMI Fifth, 2346, ZAFASAI Seventh, 7689, YALPAMB Twelfth, 9276.

19th POP
TORZOXI Twelfth, 6236, ABAIOND Eighth, 6732, OMAGRAP Eleventh, 2388.

20th KHR
ZILDRON Fifth, 3626, PARZIBA Third, 7629, TOTCAN Seventh, 3634.

21st ASP
CHIRSPA Twelfth, 5536, TOANTOM Eight, 5635, VIXPALG Sixth, 5658.

22nd LIN
OXIDAIA Twelfth, 2232, PAAOAN First, 2326, CALZIRG Twelfth, 2367.

23rd TOR
RONOAMB Seventh, 7320, ONIZIMP Seventh, 7262, ZAXANIN Eighth, 7333.

24th NIA
ORCAMIR Fourth, 8200, CHIALPS Tenth, 8360, SOAGEEL Twelfth, 8236.

25th VTI

MIRZIND Fourth, 5632, OBVAORS Second, 6333, RANGLAM Twelfth, 6236.

26th DES

POPHAND Twelfth, 9232, NIGRANA Eighth, 3620, BAZCHIM Twelfth, 5637.

27th ZAA

SAZIAMA Second, 7220, MATHULA Fourth, 7560, ORPAMB Fifth, 7263.

28th BAG

LABNIXP Tenth, 2630, FOCISNI Ninth, 7236, OXLOPAR Sixth, 8200.

29th RII

VASTRIM Third, 9632, ODRAXTI Fourth, 4236, GOMZIAM Fifth, 7635.

30th TEX

TAOAGLA Twelfth, 4632, GEMNIMB Fourth, 9636. ADVORPT Third, 7632, DOZINAL Sixth, 5632.

From these names magical Sigils are formed. But it is extremely difficult adequately to describe how the names of these 91 Princes are formed and how their Sigils are drawn. In order to avoid excessive verbiage, the following four diagrams will demonstrate clearly their Sigils drawn on the Enochian Tablets. By comparing these diagrams with the Enochian Tablets, it should be simple for the Z.A.M. to trace out these names and work out for himself the method by which they are formed from the letters of the Tablets. The customary division of Air, Fire, Water and Earth sub-elements or Lesser Angles does not enter into this matter, the Names and Sigils of the Princes, in any way whatsoever.

SIGILS OF GOVERNORS

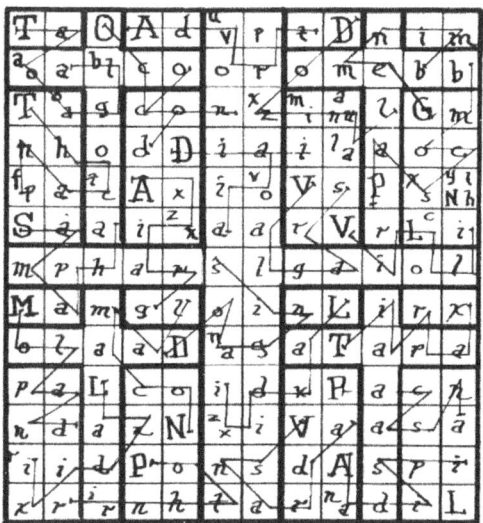

I stumbled on this formula accidentally. Later, I discovered that Crowley had worked them out years earlier, and published the Sigils in one of the Equinox volumes. I had seen this many years before my own discovery, but at this time his sigils and findings meant little to me. There are some discrepancies between Crowley's versions of the sigils and my own. Whose are more accurate, I cannot determine at this time. Nearly 50 years have elapsed since I worked on this particular problem, and my memory does not tell me much at present.

TABLETS WITH SIGILS

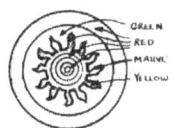

d	o	n	p	a	T	d	a	n	V	a	a
o	l	o	a	G	e	o	o	b	a	^u_v	^a_i
O	P	a	m	n	o	^v_o	G	^m_n	d	n	m
a	^P_b	l	s	T	e	^c_d	e	c	a	o	P
S	c	m	i	o	a	n	A	m	l	o	x
V	a	r	s	G	d	L	^b_v	r	i	a	P
o	i	P	t	e	a	a	p	D	o	c	e
P	s	^u_v	a	c	n	r	Z	i	r	z	a
S	i	o	d	a	o	i	n	r	z	f	m
d	a	^l_b	t	T	d	n	a	d	i	r	e
d	i	x	o	m	o	n	s	i	o	s	P
O	o	D	p	z	i	A	p	a	n	l	i
r	^d_g	o	a	n	n	^o_p	A	C	r	a	r

T	a	O	A	d	^u_v	p	t	D	n	i	m
^a_o	a	^b_l	c	o	o	r	a	m	e	b	b
T	^o_a	g	c	o	n	^x_z	^m_i	$^a_{nu}$	l	G	m
n	h	o	d	D	i	a	i	^l_a	a	o	c
^f_p	a	^t_c	A	x	i	^v_o	V	s	P	^x_s	$^{yl}_{Nh}$
S	a	a	i	^z_x	a	a	r	V	r	L^c	i
m	p	h	a	r	s	l	g	a	i	o	l
M	a	m	g	l	o	i	n	L	i	r	x
o	l	a	a	D	^n_a	g	a	T	a	p	a
p	a	L	c	o	i	d	x	P	a	c	n
n	d	a	z	N	^z_x	i	V	a	a	s	a
^r_i	i	d	P	o	n	s	d	A	s	P	i
x	r	^i_r	n	h	t	a	r	^n_a	d	i	L

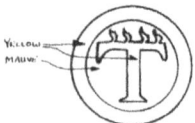

r	Z	i	l	a	f	A^y_u	t	l	i	p	a
a	r	d	Z	a	i	d	p	a	L	a	m
C	z	o	n	s	a	r	o	Y	a	u	b
T	o	i	T	t^z_x	o	P	a	c	o	C	
S	i	g	a	s	o	^n_m	r	b	z	n	h
f	m	o	n	d	a	T	d	i	a	r	l$_i$
o	r	o	i	b	a	h	a	o	z	p	i
t$_c$	N	a	b	r$_a$	V	i	x	g	a	s$_z$	d
O	i	i	i	t	T	p	a	l	O	a	i
A	b	a	m	o	o	o	a	C^u_v	c	a	
N	a	o	c	O	T	t	n	p	r	u$_a$	T
o	c	a	n	m	a	g	o	t	r	o	i
S	h	i	a	l	r	a	p	m	z	o	x

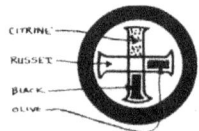

b	O	a	Z	a	R	o	P	h	a	R	a
u$_v$	N	n	a	x	o	P	S	o	n	d	n
a	i	g	r	a	n	o	a$_o$	m	a	g	g
o	r	p	m	n	i	n	g	b	e	a	l
r	s	O	n	i	z	i	r	l	e	m	u
i	z	i	n	r	C	z	i	a	M	h	l
M	O	r	d	i	a	l	h	C	t	G	a
R$_o$	C$_o$	a$_c$	$^m_{an}$	c$_m$	h$_c$	i$^{ia}_{bt}$	^s_a	o$_s$	^m_o	t$_m$	
A	r	b	i	z	m	i	l	l	p	i	z
O	p	a	n	a	B	a	m	S	m	a	T$_L$
d	O	l	o	P$_F$	l	n	i	a	n	b	a
r	x	p	a	o	c	s	i	z	i	x	p
a	x	t	i	r	V	a	s	t	r	i	m

There is very little that actually can be said about this additional tabulation which will be of any immediate practical value to the Z.A.M. If the whole scheme of the Enochian Tablets is studied in all its innumerable ramifications and an earnest endeavour made to correlate the information given here to those Tablets, then the student will discover for himself many facts of tremendous importance and significance. Unless one is well-versed in this subject, any of these matters described at greater length could appear as trivial.

But this much may be said. By studying the classical attributions of the Egyptian Gods to the squares, and by taking the Gods which are allocated to the several squares to which the Names of any of the above mentioned Governing Princes are attributed, it is possible to construct an invocation composed of the formulae of these Gods. It will comprise a species of continuous invocation of the forces of the Atziluthic world.

For example, one of the Sigils of these Princes may pass through several letters, to which squares are attributed the Goddess Isis, Nephthys, Osiris two times, Kabexnuv and Horus two times, and Hathor. An invocation of these mighty forces, vibrating their names in their Coptic attributions will serve as a most potent conjuration of the Angel whose Sigil is thus being traces.

Again, the transliteration of the letters of these Names into Hebrew makes it possible to give the correct colours from the Rose to the depicted Sigils. It will also result, by the application of conventional Order methods, in the formation likewise of Telesmatic figures of great beauty and power. All of this must be worked out personally by the Z.A.M. who finds himself interested in this system. He will be amply repaid by any expenditure of time and energy in this direction.

The Thirty Aethyrs themselves represent a scheme considerably different from what we have been able to conceptualize through the Qabalah and its major glyph of the Ten Sepiroth. It is a more primitive scheme and, bluntly, it requires a good deal of manipulation to make attributions to the Tree.

The method of application of these Keys of the Thirty Aethyrs, together with the names of their Governing Princes is extremely simple, and in part has already been shown in Ritual "T."

Let the Z.A.M. prepare the Temple as in all his ceremonies of consecration and proper working. That is, wearing his Rose-Cross lamen, with Sword and Lotus Wand at hand, implements on the altar, let him thoroughly banish all forces from his chamber, purify with water, consecrate with fire–or use the method of Opening by Watchtower. Circumambulate, and adore the Lord of the Universe. Then let the invoking Lesser Ritual of the Hexagram be performed, preceded by the Qabalistic Cross and following by the analysis of the Key-word I.N.R.I. Then let him to go to the West of the Altar, and facing East, recite the words of the Calls of the 30 Aethyrs inserting the name of whichever Aethyr he proposed to deal with.

I feel I should mention, while on this topic, that Crowley discovered, when using these Calls to cross the Abyss, that this Call which seemed a curse turned out to be–seen from the "other side of the Abyss"–a glorious paean of praise and blessing.

In the event that the Z.A.M. proposed in his skrying in the Aethyrs, to deal with the Governing Princes and Archangels, let him follow the general invocation with a particular conjuration of the Names. A slight variation could be used of the Exhortation in the Portal Grade which invokes Lexarph, Comananu and Tabitom (who are the Three Ruling Angels of the Tablet of Union as well as the 10th Aethyr ZAX) inserting in their place the Names required.

Following his skrying in the Aethyr, let the Z.A.M. reconsecrate his Temple with Fire and Water, reverse circumambulate, Adoration, and the Banishing Ritual of the Pentagram.

With regard to the Sigils that occur let it be noted that the name LAZDIXI is the only one of the 91 Names that may be attributed to the squares or letters of the Tablets, in the formation of the appropriate Sigils, in two different ways. Both are correct; the original manuscripts are silent on this matter.

Likewise, it should be noted, when the Z.A.M. works out the Sigils for himself, that the name PARAOAN forms no Sigil, and actually does not appear on any of the Tablets. I can offer no suggestion or reason why this should be so. It seems that on each of the four Tablets, there are one or two squares left over, as it were, that is, left blank after all the Sigils of the other Names have been duly drawn. The name PARAOAN is drawn from all the Tablets, and is an Angel combining the qualities of all Four Terrestrial Tablets, or synthesizes them in some way.

Moreover, be it noted that the three Angels or Princes who are shown to be the Ruling Angels over the three Divisions of the Tenth Aethyr of ZAX are also the Angels who are given as the mighty Archangels ruling over the Mystical Tablets of Union.

It is also to be noted that in invoking the Aethyr itself, the name may be transliterated into Hebrew, and vibrated while tracing its Sigil on the Rose.

PART TWO OF THE ADDENDUM TO THE BOOK OF THE CONCOURSE OF THE FORCES

(Being an exposition of the third section of the Enochian system–the Sigillum Dei Aemeth.)

One of the first important results of the ceremonial skrying of Sir Edward Kelley and Dr. John Dee was the obtaining and construction of the SIGILLUM DEI AEMETH. In this connection it is interesting to note that of these words of The Seal of the God of Truth, the word Aemeth equals the Hebrew word for Truth. And these letters reversed give us the word Thmaa (Themis), which is the name of Her who stands before the Face of the Gods in the place of the Threshold. She is the Guardian of the Hall of the Dual Manifestation of Truth. Hence, this Sigillum Dei Aemeth is one especially under her guidance and presidency.

Aleph, Mem and Tau, are the three letters representing the three elements of Air, Water and Earth. Shin representing Fire the holy spirit, is not represented directly in the name of this Sigil. However, it is implicit for the Holy spirit is Truth and overshadows the other elements of the Sigil like the brooding Spirit of God. And when the truth of the Sigil dawns on the mind, the Fire of the Spirit breaks through and illuminates the mind.

The Seal itself is a highly complex pantacle, which Dee and Kelley were instructed to make of pure wax, about 27 inches in circumference. It bears what is, at first sight, a confused medley of heptagons and heptagrams thrown in juxtaposition with innumerable crosses, numbers and letters, and a pentagram. It requires only a little attention to realize that this chaos is but a seeming one, though a good deal of careful attention is required in order to disentangle the secret of its formation. For the whole ensemble is a brilliant and highly ingenious piece of synthesis, combining diverse ideas in which all the rules of acrostics, permutations, and magical squares are alternately employed.

In the following description in these pages, it would be well to glance periodically at the Sigillum so as to be able to follow intelligently. Each step of deciphering should be referred to the reproduction of the Sigillum so that each step may be clearly understood.

Moreover, let it be remembered that the description which here follows is but a surface view of the whole, and that further meditation could disclose many other interesting and significant facts.

Around the extreme edge of the Seal's circumference is a series of numbers and letters. From these numbers, the hieroglyphs or sigils which are attributed to the Enochian Tablets may be deciphered, as shown in Ritual X. They yield the names of the Great Elemental Kings or Angel Overseers who keep guard over the Watch-Towers.

Within this circle of letters and numbers, occur seven symbols with other letters and numbers. Giving them with their formal astrological significance and Enochian names they are as follows:

1. Galas - Saturn — ♄ 5.
2. Gethog - Jupiter — ♃ 24.
3. Thaoth - Mars — ♂ 30.
4. Horlwn - Sun — ☉ 21.
5. Innon - Venus — ♀ 9.
6. Aaoth - Mercury — ☿ 14.
7. Galethog - Luna — ☽ ☉

It was after these seven planetary symbols had been dictated that one of the communicating Angels remarked significantly: "Seven rest in seven; and the seven live by seven. The seven govern the seven, and by seven all government is."

In short, this Sigillum Dei Aemeth is essentially a synthetical glyph of the septenary forces of the planets, which it analyzes at great length and with much detail in each of its several planes. The application of Order teaching–Hebrew letters, names, geomantic symbols and sigils, Tarot cards and their Dominion in the Heavens in the appropriate colours–to the skeletal form of the Dee-Kelley skrying expands it into a much more coherent and workable system. After all, precisely this was done by the original founders of the Order to the bare bones of the Four Elemental Tablets, which in their original form in the British Museum Manuscripts bear only the faintest resemblance to the comprehensive and magnificent system as developed by the Order. In providing this analysis, I shall quote from some of the alleged speeches of the communicating Angels, as some of them are of great beauty and power.

Continuing the description of the letters of the Sigillum, and working inwards from the circumference to the centre, we next find a double Heptagon, each facet of which is divided into seven compartments, each containing a letter. The point of this Heptagon is uppermost. From the diaries of Dr. Dee, it would appear that these were dictated line by line, and Kelley, the seer, would report that these letters were manifested to his vision as baskets of letters by the great Archangel Uriel. They appeared in this order:

>   Z l l R H l a
>   a Z C a a o b
>   P a u p n h r
>   h d m h i a i

The next line was communicated by putting them in this order:

The sixth basket was seen thus:

And the seventh basket in this circular form:

Now this final line or basket of letters was deemed to be of such lofty significance that Uriel uttered this fine passage: "Those seven letters are the seven Seats of the One and Ever-lasting God. His seven secret Angels proceeding from every letter and cross so formed; referred in substance to the Father; in formed to the Sonne; and inwardly to the Holy Ghost."

Incidentally, note the description of these names having reference, in the case of the substance to the Father, the form to the Son, and the inward essence to the Holy spirit, and compare it with an almost identical description given by NALVAGE in the first part of this Addendum, with reference to the Round Table which commented "Zodire Mozod Iada." It seems a characteristic of all Enochiana as it were.

"Look upon it. It is one of the Names which thou hast before; every letter containing an Angel of Brightness; comprehending the seven inward powers of God, known to none but Himself. A sufficient BOND to urge all creatures to Life or Death, or anything else contained in this world. It banishes the wicked, expelleth evil spirits, qualifieth the Waters, strengtheneth the Just, exalteth the righteous, and destroyeth the wicked. He is One in Seven. He is twice Three. He is Seven in the whole. He is almighty. His name is everlasting; His truth cannot fail. His glory is incomprehensible. Blessed be His name. Blessed be Thou, O God, for ever."

By putting the above letters together in seven ordered lines, in the form of a square, we obtain the following figure. The Angel further remarked of this arrangement that "every letter containeth or comprehendeth the number of 72 virtues. "It is important to recall that 72 equals the number of Angels of the Quinaries, the Shem-hamphoresh.

For convenience sake, we will label this figure as the Archangelic Square.

Z	l	l	R	H	i	a
a	Z	C	a	a	c	b
P	a	u	P	n	h	r
h	d	m	h	i	a	i
K	K	a	a	e	e	e
i	i	e	e	l	l	l
e	e	l	l	M	G	✠

Beginning with the letter Z in the upper left hand corner and reading all the way down the file, and including the first letter of the second horizontal file, we find spelled the name of Zaphkiel the Archangel of Binah and the Sphere of Saturn. Beginning with the Z on the second line and following a similar procedure, the result turns out to be Zadkiel, the Archangel of Chesed, and the Sphere of Tzedek or Jupiter. Then follow, commencing in each instance with an upper case letter, Camael, the Archangel of Geburah and the Sphere of Madim, Mars; Raphael the Archangel of Shemesh, Sun; Haniel the Archangel of Netzach and the sphere of Nogah, Venus; Michael the Archangel of Hod, and the sphere of Kokab, Mercury; and Gabriel, the Archangel of Yesod, and the sphere of Levanah, the Moon.

Malkuth is symbolized, without any other attribution or description, by the concluding Cross, and in Enochian symbolism, as Ritual X testifies, the Cross is always read as "th" as Tau the letter of Earth. And the idea of Earth as the epitomization of the foregoing names is further suggested by the fact that the whole figure is to be constructed of wax. Moreover, on the reverse side of the Sigillum Dei Aemeth, Malkuth is further summarized by this figure:

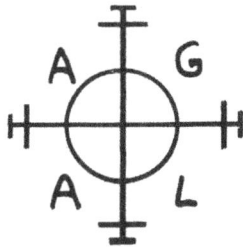

AGLA, a notariqon of "Thou art mighty forever, O Lord." And AGLA, be it noted, is the Name of Power vibrated to the North in the Lesser Ritual of the Pentagram.

This completes one way of reading the letters in the Square. As the archangel Uriel said, however, in the above-mentioned quotation, there are several ways of viewing these letters in the formation of Names. I content myself for the moment with the above, leaving to the Z.A.M. the task of further working out these mysteries in the light of what has already been stated.

Before proceeding to the next part of the Sigillum, I must record another Angelic speech, this time made by Michael: "Mark this Mystery. Seven comprehendeth the Secrets of Heaven and Earth. Seven knitteth man's soul and body together (three in Soul and four in body.) In seven thou shalt find the Unity. In Seven thou shalt find the Trinitie. In seven thou shalt find the sum and proportion of the Holy Ghost. O God, O God, O God. Thy Name, O God, be praised ever, from Thy seven thrones, from Thy seven trumpets, and from Thy Seven Angels, Amen, Amen, Amen!"

Immediately under the Heptagon described above, there will be seen on the Sigillum seven sets of upper-case letters and figures.

These figures and letters are organized in a square on a later page.

These names comprise, according to the Angel "seven names of God, not known to the angels, neither can they be spoken of or read of man. These Names bring forth Seven Angels (1), the governors of the heavens next unto us. Every letter of the Angels' names bringeth forth seven daughters (2). Every daughter bringeth forth her daughter (3); every daughter her daughter bringeth forth a son (4). Every son hath his son (5)." This would apparently indicate that there are five sets of hierarchical names. In the Order system, five relates to the letters of the Pentagrammaton, Yod Heh Shin Vau Heh equals the five elements. Each set of names therefore is attributable to the five elements, ruling the four Elemental Tablets and the Tablet of Union.

In the form above given, certainly it would appear that as names they cannot be spoken of or read by man. But by reference to the letters on the extreme circumference of the Sigillum, we find that 21 is E, 8 is L; also 30 is L. Thus by interpolating these letters instead of keeping the numbers, we acquire SAAIELEMEL, and BTZKASEL, etc. This makes the names a little less impossible to use, and by employing the now familiar rules of Enochian pronunciation, that is of vibrating each letter separately, a fairly sonorous vibration is obtained. These are the Divine Names ruling the spheres of the planets.

By treating these letters in much the same way as the former series, a similar square is obtained. This we shall call the Angelic Square to differentiate it from the Archangelic.

S	A	A	I_8^{21}	E	M	E	VENIT IN COELIS
B	T	Z	K	A	S	E	DUES NOSTER
H	E	I	D	E	N	E	DUX NOSTER
D	E	I	M	O	30	A	HIC EST
I^{26}	M	E	G	C	B	E	LUX IN AETERNUM
I	L	A	O	I_8^{21}	V	N	FINIS EST
I	H	R	L	A	A	$_8^{21}$	VERA EST HAEC TABULA

The mode of reading these letters is slightly different from that previously demonstrated. It is easier to describe it by tracing a Sigil than to use a large number of words, and I again give the square below with a line drawn in ink to show the procedure to be adopted.

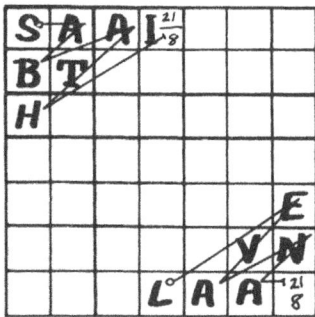

If the same process is continuously followed, commencing immediately after each number, the Z.A.M. will obtain the following:

Sabathiel - the Angel ruling the sphere of Saturn.
Zedekiel - the Angel ruling the sphere of Jupiter.
Madimiel - the Angel ruling the sphere of Mars.
Semeliel - the Angel ruling the sphere of Sol.

There is an undoubted mistake occurring at this juncture. If these letters and names were dictated, then Kelley must have wrongly heard and written an L where S was intended in last name. The name involved is actually Semesiel–since Semes or Shemesh is the Hebrew word for Sun. However, if one changes this letter on the square, the effects obviously are far-reaching, for it changes also many other names obtained by means of other modes of permutation. This I have not cared to do, beyond noting the existence of the error.

Nogahiel - the Angel ruling the sphere of Venus.
Korabiel - the Angel ruling the sphere of Mercury.

Here again is an error, one no doubt more of vision than of hearing, in this instance. R is recorded where K is quite evidently intended. The name of Mercury in Hebrew is Kokab not Korab - therefore the angelic name should be Kokabiel.

Levanael - the Angel of the sphere of the Moon.

Here clearly we have the beginning of a hierarchical system. God names have already been given, together with symbols of planets and the Enochian names of these spheres. Now we have Archangels and Angels, with servient hierarchies hereafter to be noted.

Referring back to the Angelic Square again, let me demonstrate a second method of permutation. Below I give the square again, let me demonstrate a second method of permutation. Below I give the square again, with a line drawn diagonally from top left to bottom right to indicate the procedure to be followed. This yields the name STIMCUL.

A similar process is to be employed for all other squares that is by drawing diagonal Name. This then yields BEIGIA, HEEOA, DMAL, ILI, IH, I. On the right of the first name, you will find AZDOBN, AKELE, IANA, ESE, ME, EL.

Should we refer to the Rose of the Z.A.M., we can make formal Sigils of their power in their true magical colours, as follows:

ANGELIC SIGIL

By referring to the Order document on Telesmatic Images, it will become evident that these letters may be used to call up telesmatic figures of no little beauty. Another mode of analysis can be pursued by taking the Gematria of the name AZDOBN, which in this case equals 720, (72x10) and by subjecting it to the Qabalah of Nine Chambers, as shown by a very similar technique with regard to the Sephiroth in Ritual "M" we obtain Gemini and Mercury. The name is thus clearly of a mercurial nature, with an octagram as its lineal figure, attributed to the Sphere of Hod, under the presidency of ELOHIM TZABAOTH, and in forming a telesmatic image, this idea should be carried into practice. Note too that its first two letters AZ are those of AZBOGAH, on of the Mercury Names.

Leaving these names for a moment, and referring back once more to the diagram of the Sigillum Dei Aemeth, we see that after the Unpronounceable Names of God which we obtained and formed into a square, there appears next a double Heptagram, point upwards, and inside this a double Heptagon with a facet upwards and point down. Within the points and borders of these lineal figures are further names and letters–four lines or separate divisions, in fact. If the Zelator Adeptus Minor refers to these, he will find around the seven-pointed figures, beginning with the uppermost names as follows: EL, ME, ESE, IANA, AKELE, AZDOBN, STIMCUL. (These should be written in both upper and lower case letters, though for legibility here I am using capitals only.) The second set of names beginning from the top is: I, HEEOA, IL, BEIGIA, ILI, STIMCUL, DMAL.

Quite clearly these are names derived from the square by the second method of permutation, and we have now shown how these names were obtained, and whence they derive.

Let us apply a third method of permutation. This mode is similar to the second, except that it works from right top downwards to bottom left. The square is as below, and a diagonal line shows the name ESEMELI.

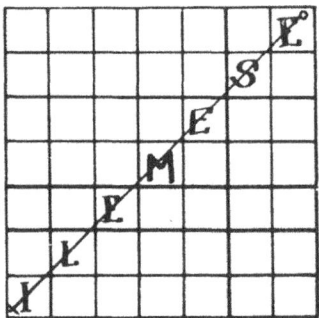

The names yielded by this method are, on the left: MADIMIEL, EKIEI, IZED, ATH, AB, S. This set of seven names are the third series within the Heptagon on the Sigillum, immediately beneath or within those listed before.

Going back to our method of presenting the diagonal permutations of the Square, but this time working from the bottom upwards, we obtain on the right side: ILEMESE, HAGONEL, IOCLE, LIBE, AVE, AN, EL. These also will be found to be the final set of names enclosed by the Heptagon.

Two things should here be noted. The first is, that in Ritual "T," which is the Book of the 48 Calls, there is a reference to

Irwin's manuscript which was alleged to have given certain names. Reference to the page whereon this occurs, will disclose the fact that some of the above-mentioned names are those referred to. Some of the others, however, I cannot place, such as GALVAH, MURFIRI, NAPSAMA, NALVAGE. I am not able to work out whence they derive, though all are names which figure prominently in the record of the Dee-Kelley skrying. Evidently they belong to one of the other systems–to the Round Table of Nalvage, or the Heptarchia Mystica.

Incidentally, note that the name Ave occurs, and that our tradition asserts that the Terrestrial or Elemental Tablets are delivered unto Enoch by the great Angel Ave.

Secondly, it will now fully be understood why I have not ventured to correct what appeared to be two mistakes. If on the big Angelic Square I have altered certain letters so as to produce accuracy in the spelling of KORABIEL and SEMELIEL, which are obviously incorrect, the alteration would entail similar changes in the names of at least four other angelic names. And the responsibility for doing this is too great for me to assume. It does suggest however a profitable and worthwhile field of research for the Z.A.M. who has more experience in skrying and astral projection.

To complete the analysis of the Sigillum, let it be noted that the centre consists of a double Pentagram, enclosing a cross. The letters there will be seen to be the hierarchical names obtained from the Angels of the Planets with the Angel of Saturn. SABATHIEL, enclosing the others, as though to affirm the supernal and general nature of Saturn, as corroborated by the Ritual of the Hexagram, where the Saturn Hexagram is said to call forth the general powers of the Macrocosm. Within the enclosing sphere of Sabathiel, are the Angels of Tzedek, Madim, Shemesh, Nogah, and Kokab, arranged about the points of the Pentagram. The initial capital letters of these five planets are placed within the point or angle itself, the remaining letters being spaced out from point to point. In the centre, placed about the arms of the Cross, receiving the influence of all, is the name of Levanael, the Angel of the Moon. The synthesis of them all is the Earth.

Enough now has been stated concerning this matter of Names, and the Z.A.M. with a little application can work out other series of names, in various combinations, for himself.

One more important point should be noticed. Inasmuch as the Book of the Concourse of the Forces states that the names of the Six Seniors and the King of each Tablet, attributed to the points of the Hexagram, represent the operation of the Planets through the elemental world, the Z.A.M. should employ, when working with the names of the King and Six Seniors. For this reason, that the names on the Sigillum represent the root and source of the forces which in the Terrestrial Watch-Towers are mixed and compounded with the elements. And the true attribution of the names of the King and Six Seniors to the planets is:

King, the central whorl on the Cross, to the Sun.

The names on the left half of the Linea Spiritus Sancti to Mars.

The names of the right half of the Linea Spiritus Sancti to Venus.

The name on the upper left half of the Linea Patris to Jupiter.

The name on the lower half of the Linea Dei Patris to Mercury.

The name on the upper half of the Linea Dei Filiique to Moon.

The name on the lower half of the Linea Dei Filiique to Saturn.

This completes the description of the form of, and the names upon, the Siggilum Dei Aemeth. The Heptarchia Mystica continues the same magical theme, as it were, by listing the 49 Angelorum Bonorum, and their servient ministers, who are under the governance of the Angels whose Names are shown in the Heptagon of the Sigillum. For instance, HAGONEL, is described as presiding over, within his particular sphere of government, a king named CARMARA and a Prince named BAREES, under whom are 42 ministers, to whose commandment the Sons of Light are subject. And the invocation of these 49 Good Angels are the contents of Liber Logaeth, a description of which, together with a summary of the Heptarchical Mystery, will comprise the third section of this Addendum, (which I have not had the time to finish.)

There appears, on the surface, to be no relationship existing between the names given in Part I of this Addendum and those on the Sigillum and those on the Tablets comprising the Round Table of Nalvage. They occupy different planes, with different characteristics.

DISCUSSION OF THE Z-DOCUMENTS

(These three document, Z-1, Z-2, and Z-3, are amongst the most important of all the instructions issued by the Golden Dawn. They are extensive commentaries on the Neophyte Ritual. All these are replete with the most profound instruction on Magic ever written.

As I reflect upon what I have written in this book I am sure that I have asserted several times that this particular document or that one are the most important lessons ever released within the Order. This is probably most correct. All the instructions handed out to the Zelator Adeptus Minor are unequivocally important in different ways. But they all serve as the foundation of the magical art. Throughout the years, whenever, I have casually opened the book to any page of these Z documents, I have found them always illuminating–more so with each perusal of their contents. Their ability to illuminate seems inexhaustible. And for this reason, I must insist that the student pay special attention to them, studying them carefully over a long period of time rather than trying to read them as he would a novel or some informative non-fictional piece of work.

They have all the earmarks of having been written by S.L. Mathers–G.H. Frater D.D.C.F. More than anything else I know, they exemplify the profundities of which he was capable.

Admittedly some of the material is trite, elaborating the usual claptrap of secret societies–such as grips, steps and passwords. But these trivia comprise but a small segment of these fantastic papers. The remaining material is of such a nature that I feel compelled to warn the casual reader not to be casual in dealing with this type of information. This is "heavy" material which needs to be savored, thought about and reflected upon.

For example, in the description of the accoutrements of the Hierophant, one is inclined to gloss it over as merely explanatory of the Temple equipment. It is really much more than that. Some formulae of magic were concealed and simultaneously revealed in the most prosaic and trite explanations and descriptions. Do not gloss over them.

From the standpoint of practical magical technique, I suggest a frequent review of the segment entitled "The Symbolism of the Opening." One practical formula after another is described here, not abstractly but concretely as a technical exercise available to the alert and eager aspirant.

Some of these served as seminal ideas which came to full term in the development of the Middle Pillar technique. The rudiments are all Golden Dawn. But each rudiment is scattered here and there, throughout several documents. However, one does not really have to search too hard for them. They are prolific–presenting themselves as alive and vital. Over a period of time, as one uses them, the seeds sprout and grow into dynamic constituents of one's wake-a-day consciousness as though waiting to be found and used.

For example, there was the rudimentary Middle Pillar technique as given in one of the early Portal papers. The technique of circulating the energies awakened or released by this method of meditation are to be found in part in this particular paper. It is only a hint, however. It becomes rounded out and expanded by applying that idea to the formula of the Tree of Life projected into a sphere, producing four individual columns around a central invisible pillar. The roots of all this will be found in the Microcosm paper and elsewhere, but in its fullness in those documents at the end of the Tarot section.

The attributions of the planets, signs and houses are standard astrological notions within the Golden Dawn system. Its employment as described, for example, in *The Foundations of Practical Magic* Aquarian Press, 1979 depends entirely on how well one has understood and used some of the principles of that magical exercise.

The technique has been borrowed without acknowledgment by a number of writers who believed it to be a magical technique borrowed from the Order. In a large sense, they were plagiarizing, because in no place has this method been described except in the barest outline form. Yet in a sense which they never realized, because they were actually plagiarizing, it is predicated fundamentally and unequivocally on the whole basic structure of the Golden Dawn system itself. And it is that system that hostile critics claim was the end result of research done by McGregor Mathers in the British Museum. If taken by itself, it is pure nonsense. I defy any critic to demonstrate where and how these methods were borrowed from books or manuscripts in the British Museum.

In The Symbolism of the Opening, there is given first the method of vibrating Divine Names. It is called The Vibratory Formula of the Middle Pillar. Again, I must urge the student to study it carefully. It has been repeated and elaborated upon in several different places in these texts. But you must study it, practise it and master it.

Once mastered, it should be used in all instances where the Divine Names are employed. These are in the practice of the Pentagram Ritual, lesser and greater, the Hexagram Ritual, lesser and greater, and the Middle Pillar technique itself, (Note, some of these rituals are described in the *Regardie Tapes* Falcon Press, 1982). These tapes can help enormously in the mastery of the various ceremonials themselves–such as the consecration of the Elemental Weapons, and so on. The method of pronouncing and vibrating the Names is clearly indicated on the Tapes so as to eliminate all possibilities of doubt and confusion.

Some techniques too are infinitely valuable during the process of skrying. Safeguards are required here to protect one from delusion and self-deception–all too easy in this method. The use of the Banners of the East and West may also be used as devices to open up areas that one would not suspect could be opened, so securely are they guarded.

The assumption of God-forms described in several of these documents, which comment on the Neophyte Ritual is another method of not merely of protecting oneself, but of ensuring compliance with one's demands for knowledge and self-knowledge, and for gaining admission to sanctuaries whose existence one may suspect–but that is all.

This practice needs to be used often to gain skill. The descriptions given in the text are brief enough as well as long enough. That is really all it requires. Once having made its acquaintance, nothing remains but to practice it day in and day out until it is more or less easy. One of the best books that gives practically all the needed God-forms is the paperback reprint by Dover of Wallis Budge's *The Gods of Egyptians*. This is not only a storehouse of Egyptian information, but the dozens of full page plates of the Gods is without rival in our literature. At the same time for a better descriptions of the colours employed in the God Forms, you should consult the colour plates in this book.

The section in Z-1 describing the God forms used in the Neophyte initiation will be more than amplify what has just been stated. Those colors used in the first edition of Budge's book by Methuen, decades ago, are accurate enough in terms of how they were once depicted. But for practical uses, the colour scheme shown in this work is to be preferred. Never let it be forgotten that one of the basic themes of the Order is that colors are not symbols of forces, but are focuses themselves. So do study the coloring system and apply it to the plain photos of the Dover edition.

There are hosts of fertile ideas in these papers. I do not wish to elaborate all of them in any way. Something must be left to the ingenuity and intuition of the reader and student. But what I have had to say here should be adequate to keep him alert when perusing this most valuable and suggestive series of texts.

One of the many documents given to advanced members of the Zelator Adeptus Minor grade was Z-2, an elaborate analysis of the Neophyte grade. The breakdown into a couple of dozen specific points, is in itself, one of the most beautiful and astute tabulations I know. Like so many of the Adeptus Minor papers, it fills me with enormous respect for whoever was responsible for the analysis. The entire elaboration was classified into five major divisions, corresponding to the Pentagrammaton. In addition, that section attributed to Shin was broken down still further into three other segments so that all told there were seven formulae for magical working.

Z-2 was one of the papers that was destined for elimination from the curriculum of the Stella Matutina, a most grave error. My guess is that it was being eliminated because it represented some exceedingly hard work on the part of the celebrant.

The application of Z-2 to the process of Divination was never quite clear to me. Rather than follow the procedure of the Stella Matutina, I have decided to include it here because some students will be able to determine on their own what its sphere of usefulness is. If the student follows the general rule laid down for all the other subdivisions of this important document, he may arrive at some format pleasing and useful to him personally.

The Alchemy section for long years bothered me, for I am not able to make much sense from it. Francis King, in his book Ritual Magic in England reproduces a paper based on this section. It is most interesting, but raises an enormous number of questions relating to procedure, laboratory technique and allied topics. I had some correspondence with Mr. King about this matter but nothing came of it.

Sometime during the mid-thirties some alchemical processes became more or less clear to me, which made more intelligible some of the sections in Z-2. Years later, after a meeting with Frater Albertus of the Paracelsus Research Society, new insights developed.

A ritual exemplifying the rules laid down in Z-2 will be found immediately following the various initiatory rituals.

So far as rituals relating to evocation and similar types of operations are concerned some students found out that they are long, tedious, repetitive and very wearying. I must confess they are. Success in working them depends on patience, enthusiasm, and above all on the ability to stir the magical energy into activity. The rituals themselves will not yield much satisfaction until and unless the student has either some inborn theurgic ability or has developed it through the practice of the Middle Pillar technique.

The method awakens the magical centers or chakras within the psycho-spiritual make-up of the student, a process of prime importance, because without the power derived from these centers or chakras, the ritual remains merely a ritual–a mere formality, dead and without power. The Middle Pillar should be practiced for several months, or even longer, until the student becomes thoroughly conscious of the energy coursing through the organism at his willed command in the three methods of circulation. The sensation is unmistakable, becoming wholly physical if steadfastly persisted in. It is the sine qua non of magical success.

When some skill has been gained in this method, further attention can be given to the Vibratory Formula of the Middle Pillar, described in several places in this work. The success of any of these operations is wholly dependent on these two methods, the Middle Pillar and the Vibratory Formula, and they should be given a great deal of attention.

When this material was first published many years ago, one of the gratifying rewards was hearing from a few students who evidently had experimented with the method. One in particular stands out. I would have liked to acknowledge his contribution, but for the moment he wishes to remain anonymous. His letter gives evidence of the fact that he has experimented with the method and found it, for him, wanting, so that he felt obliged to clarify the procedure and simplify it. His complaint was that the whole ceremony took approximately two hours, at the end of which time he felt exhausted and was unable to retain any kind of "divine intoxication" which is the sine qua non of success. The method which he then devised is as follows:

"The magician, standing in the circle, performs a banishing ritual. (For the evocation of an elemental, the lesser Pentagram ritual will suffice. If evoking a more powerful spirit, use the

Supreme Banishing Ritual of the Pentagram, or Hexagram, as appropriate.)

"A suitable God is invoked. Assumption of God form, Vibratory Formula of the Middle Pillar, and Mystic Circumambulation being employed. This is continued until presence of the Divine Force is unmistakable; one ought to have the impression of acting on behalf of the God.

"The Sigil of the Spirit is now consecrated and placed in the Triangle outside the Circle. The element, planetary, or zodiacal force consonant with the nature of the spirit is invoked using the proper Pentagram or Hexagram, Divine Names, etc.

"Invocation of the God is recommenced and continued until identity with the God is achieved. At this point the actual evocation may begin. (The Magician will hereafter be referred to as the God.)

"The God extends His consciousness up to the spirit's plane (not unlike skrying), formulates its sigil therein, calls its name.

"The Spirit is commanded to manifest in the Triangle, and as the God brings his consciousness back into the body of the magician in the circle, the spirit manifests in the triangle.

"When he has sworn allegiance, and answered all questions put to him, he is commanded to return to his own plane. The God again extends His consciousness up to the plane, bringing the spirit with Him. When they have both arrived, the Sigil previously formulated is banished.

"He returns to the Circle, then partially withdraws from the magician, who again becomes aware that he is acting on behalf of the God.

"The element, planetary or zodiacal force previously invoked, is now banished. The magician then performs a general banishing ritual and quits the circle."

The writer of the above method adds a note, which in my opinion is worth paying close attention to; it coincides with my own view as expressed elsewhere.

"There is reason for concern that students may misinterpret certain of Crowley's magical writings. For example in *Magick in Theory and Practice*, Chapter IX, p. 69, he writes:

'The peculiar mental excitement required may even be aroused by the perception of the absurdity of the process, and the persistence in it, as when Frater Perdurabo…recited **From Greenland's Icy Mountains** and obtained his result.'"

"Now there is no doubt that the ego, excited to the proper pitch, is capable of placing such a strain in the Astral Light as to cause some sort of manifestation, perhaps even that of the spirit it was desired to evoke (but more likely a phantasm masquerading as such). But without the presence of the Divine Force, such a being, once evoked, cannot be controlled, and there is no effective means of banishing it.

"Depending on the nature of the spirit, and the degree of its manifestation, it is likely that the spiritual progress of the magician is at an end–at least as far as his current incarnation is concerned."

While on this topic of magical training and developing the powers latent in man, to which the Order is dedicated, I would like to quote extensively from another source. Though the Theosophical Society is to all intents and purposes dead, there is some pertinent material in *The Hall of Magic Mirrors* by Victor Endersby that should set most of us back on our heels and induce some deep reflection. The tradition is a different one but facts are facts regardless of where they come from. In discussing the problem of psychical phenomena produced by Madame Blavatsky, Mr. Endersby had this to say:

"The crux of the whole problem is that the whole movement had to balance on a razor edge between credence and incredulity; and a net had to be spread whose meshes were designed, with infinite care, to catch fish or just a certain size and shape. Unfortunately, even a Mahatma could not design one which would exclude a particularly odd member of the species–the one known variously as "crackpot," "screwball," "oddball," etc. These have been especially effective shields, but also especially irritating ones. Some of the most enthusiastic devotees of Theosophy would convince any sane-minded man in five minutes that there could not possibly be anything real in it.

However, let us not be too hard on the gentle crackpot. After all, through the ages most human progress has depended on his existence–he is the one who is reckless enough to crack the ice with no thought of consequences, any more than of reason, common sense, and facts. Most really capable and competent people have, by those qualities, established a position in the world, which they will not readily risk in pioneering. The risks have in the main to be left to people without sense enough to be afraid, and they serve their purpose in their odd ways. After all, some of them have made quite a splash here and there. Considering him from the purely personal aspect, what else would you call Einstein? Or a certain famous gentleman who choose to immure himself in an African jungle and lavish his gifts on a minor collection of ignorant natives?

We will examine the meshes of the occult net.

The Mahatma said that chelaship was impossible to anyone who harbors any tendency toward injustice, even unconsciously. First then, do you love scandal and ill talk, unverified and one-sided about others? If so, you are out, and the famous scandals will take you out.

Are you a coward, afraid to stand up for justice? If so, you will keep silent in the face of slander. That will take you out. There is no room for cowards beyond the veil.

Do you still have the ecclesiastic notion that perfection and infallibility can exist in an ever-evolving universe? Then your misconception of the universe is profound, probably incurable; a few scientific, grammatical, or philosophical errors will set you out on the doorstep.

Are you a materialist, unable to grasp even the possibility that the real universe is not a material one? Then the phenomena will be self-evident fraud to you, and that will take you out. You will also get out with your sanity, because the escape hatches have been left; and the victims will be fairly safe from harm because, instead of striking matches, you will only laugh at them.

Do you wish to set yourself up to be admired as an Infallible One by acquiring much knowledge? Then the revelation of fallible possibilities on the parts of the highest "authorities" you know–if you are a Theosophist–will set you back a little, and possibly out. And if you twist and squirm in the effort to prove the infallibility of your gods, that identifies your degree of intellectual honesty. That's the sort of thing they want to know.

Are you prejudiced racially and nationally? Then the program of universal brotherhood will steer you far away.

Are you narrow-minded, fastidious, finicky, and given to taking the form for the substance? Then a little swearing will take care of you.

Are you mentally lazy? Then the effort to untangle those peculiar books and make sense of them will take adequate care of you. No mentally lazy person can understand the occult world, let alone the visible one.

Are your interests narrow? Then the help you will need from all available human sources won't be there–you are uninterested in too much of it. You will find yourself in one blind alley or the other.

Do you think the kingdom of heaven can be gained by physical observances, and that a meat-eater is a lower animal? Then a few eggs in gravy will eliminate you nicely; if that won't do it, a few packs of cigarettes will take care of it. Especially when you find that one of the Mahatmas smoked a pipe.

It has often been asked, why, with all the resources and wisdom of the Mahatmas, was H.P.B. left to struggle in poverty and illness? As we have seen, she was accused–though no individual ever came forward to complain–of getting rich on the credulity of her followers. Suppose she had been richly maintained? Moncure Conway, the missionary, mentions her "richly furnished" apartment. No doubt the furniture had been expensive–before her wealthy friends gave it to her when they got new stuff. She never starved for food, that is certain; she always did have enough–money–to do what she had to do. As to health–we can lay that in part to herself. She did break all the rules of diet, and possibly not all because of thyroid trouble and the rest; she was a hardheaded, intractable party. She knew all the rules. If she chose to break them, the Mahatmas couldn't do anything about it. Of course, they could have "fired" her, but then she was the only agent able to do what they had in mind.

The queer thing about these questions is that they are often from Christians, whose own God left his only Son to live in hardship and poverty and die in horror.

If you have to test out the morals of a tribe of savages, to see whether it is ready to haul its snout out of the mud and take the road to civilization, a good way is to drop a sick child of the same race but another tribe into the village compound. They may kill it with a club, throw it on the fire, torture it with sharp sticks, eat it, or pick it up and care for it. If they do anything but the last, you leave–quickly–and wait a hundred years until the tribe has outgrown its land and impinged on the territory of a bigger one. It may then appreciate help. Meanwhile, if you are interested in technical educability, you string a phone wire and show that you can talk over it. The natives decide that you are a god. You show them that you can't crawl through the wire–you're a fake. You then decide that they will have to mature a little before you try to teach them electricity. They will grasp one use of the wire very quickly; it will make good necklaces, when cut up, or good slugs for the blunderbuss.

Of course, in order to get their attention in the first place, you have to either shoot some of them, or display a cigarette lighter. If they have not caught on by the time the fluid runs out, you run out too. And stay a long time."

SELF-INITIATION

The Neophyte Ritual and that of the Adeptus Minor Grade are the most important and effective rituals of the Order. Those in between are the so-called elemental rituals. Crowley took a rather dim view of these. Francis King assumed wrongly that I also held much the same attitude. In fact, however, I think that they have a very definite place in the entire process of initiation. That they are verbose and overlong I will admit to. Nonetheless there are ways and means of overcoming this problem. In my recently published book *Ceremonial Magic* (Aquarian Press, England) a ritual opening that I called Opening by Watchtower (first demonstrated in the consecration ceremony of the Vault of the Adepts) could be elaborated meaningfully in a variety of different ways which could be construed as effective as abbreviated elemental initiations.

To be concise, an elemental initiation is one in which the elementals are invoked in such a way that they affect the sphere of sensation or the energy field of the candidate. A series of impressions or symbols are impressed on this energy field in such a way that they act, for the candidate, as a kind of passport providing safe entry and freedom of movement in that elemental sphere of operation.

Assuming that this is the case, then the four elemental grade initiations of the Outer Order, in reality do little more than the abbreviated Opening by Watchtower ceremonies. A number of advantages flow from this assumption. The first is that the ritual is nowhere as turgid, lengthy and tiresome as is the grade ritual, all criticisms which led Crowley and others to the faulty conclusion that they could be dispensed with as useless. The second, and I think most important one, is that the Watchtower rituals described in the book named above could be employed as self-initiatory rituals.

Again, assuming that this is factual, then we have reached a stage which fulfills the original promise of some of my early writings on the Golden Dawn–which was that since the Hermetic Order of the Golden Dawn was now defunct, the isolated student here, there and everywhere, could now be his own initiator. This does not preclude the possibility that new temples might arise and have arisen in various parts of the world independently of any other temple. Several new temples have in recent years been formulated and are functioning very successfully, with new temples emerging even now.

In stating that the isolated student could now be his own initiator, one important phrase is rendered imperative. And that is he must be persistent and as thoroughgoing and exacting as if he were an initiator in a regularly constituted Golden Dawn temple under the constant scrutiny of officialdom and higher adept authorities. The responsibility for progress is thus placed inexorably on the student or candidate himself. As I see it–and I have watched this on a very few students–each elemental initiation or Watchtower ceremony requires its repetition several times. One student whom I am thinking of at this juncture has performed the whole Opening by Watchtower ceremonies some 50 or 60 times. It is therefore my opinion that she has initiated herself as effectively and as positively as any temple initiatory hierophantic team could possibly do. All the important "command" symbols of elemental significance are altogether imbedded in her aura or energy field so that should she visit their sphere of activity, via skrying in the spirit vision, they would not regard her as an enemy alien invading their hallowed circle. Instead, she would be regarded as friendly and as a divine helper because she carries, as it were, the only correct and valid passport recognized by them as an official password.

The only and still major problem remaining as of this moment is how to convert the Neophyte and Adeptus Minor rituals into self-initiatory operations. I am willing to write off the Adeptus Minor ritual as impossible to convert to a self-initiatory ceremony. It still requires an authentic initiator to accomplish the purpose of this ritual. I see no possibility of converting this, as things stand at this moment.

However, I still feel that the Neophyte ritual does contain the possibilities of conversion. It has been done in other ways. For example Crowley, while in Mexico, did one series of meditations, almost tantric in nature, that utilized the clairvoyant visions of G.H. Frater S.R.M.D. The latter did describe in Z-1 and Z-3 what happened to the candidate during the Neophyte initiation in full temple ceremonies. This I described in my biography of Aleister Crowley, *The Eye In the Triangle*, Falcon Press, 1982. (Although some students dislike Crowley the study of his life and the effect of the Golden Dawn on him is essential to our understanding of extending the work of the Order.) Years later, when he came to full term as an initiator himself, he wrote a book of instruction entitled *Liber HHH* (included in *Gems from the Equinox*, Falcon Press, 1982). In one section of that Liber he refined his early meditation and created a magnificent instruction. This also I have quoted in *The Eye In the Triangle*. However, I am not looking in that direction at this particular moment. What I wish to do is so to simplify the Neophyte ritual as practiced in the Order, by deleting a number of segments which are not necessarily integral to the process of initiation. And leaving a ceremonial skeleton which can be adapted by any student to the service of his own initiation. For example, the entire section in which the various officers give speeches describing what some of the symbols amount to and furthermore name the various subjects that must be studied by the candidate before he can be advanced further in the Order. This would eliminate a good deal of unnecessary baggage and shorten the ritual the student would have to learn. It is quite likely too that most of the opening of the temple in the Neophyte grade could also be left out without harm to the entire initiatory process–with the exception of that passage of the Hierophant which stated that by names and symbols are all powers awakened and re-awakened. Whether the circumambulations should be omitted I have yet to decide, on the basis of some experimentation myself. Much the same applies to the purification by water and the consecration by fire–processes which are repeated several times.

This then leaves as the most important part of the ritual the obligation at the Altar, the charge of the Hierophant to quit the night and seek the day, the reception into the Order and the Hegemon's guiding the newly initiated Neophyte between the two pillars between the altar and the station of the East.

It was only when discussing this matter with V.H. Soror Sic Itur Ad Astra in Los Angeles recently that some light was shed on this problem. The core of the solution revolved around the notion that initiation outside of a regularly constituted Temple was only possible with two students. They would have to prove to themselves–not to anyone else–that they were wholly devoted to the Great Work, devoted enough to spend at least several months jointly or individually practising the Middle Pillar technique as described in *The Foundation of Practical Magic*, Aquarian Press, 1979. If this practice were assiduous and intense both students would have awakened in themselves the psycho-spiritual energy that could not only hasten their own inner development but that the latter could be communicated to yet another in a manner not too dissimilar to that described in Z-3.

The fundamental requirement was that the initiator should be an initiator–not a layman out of the brute herd. Something must have happened to him to have redeemed him of the stigma of being "ordinary." Of course it would have been better if he (or she) had been the recipient of a spontaneous mystical experience of the type described in James' *Varieties of Religious Experience*. Since this kind of attainment cannot be made to order, as it were, the only alternative is to fall back on time honored methods of development and growth.

I am well aware of the debate which has gone on for years as to whether mystical or occult practices can induce the mystical experience–conversion or samadhi or satori, call it what you will. If not, then it is maintained that these practices prepare the student for that possibility if not inducing it actually. And if he have patience to "wait upon the Lord," as it were, then the one is as good as the other, from my point of view.

While pursuing their work with the Middle Pillar technique and any other set of exercises to which they may be drawn, they could set themselves to the task of studying the Neophyte Ritual and the Z documents that pertain to it. There is additional suggestive material in this topic in *The Eye In the Triangle*. Using the clairvoyant description given by Mathers of what really happened between the Two Pillars to the candidate, Crowley developed a meditation incorporating all those ideas, as I have intimated above. Apparently this meditation must have proven successful, for many years later after he had come to term he wrote a document for his own Order, the A∴A∴, known as *Liber HHH*. The first section of this document elaborates this meditation and transforms the clairvoyant description of Mathers into an extraordinary piece of magical work that has fascinated me for many years for as long as I have known of the *Equinoxes* that he published as long ago as 1909-1914.

All of this could give them ideas and hints as to how to proceed in the task of initiating themselves or others. First one and then another could be helped to come to the Light in much the same way as if they were operating in a duly constituted Temple. In fact, to go one further, there is no reason why the officers of a regular Temple should not follow some such procedure as this themselves. It would certainly do no harm, and in fact would accomplish a great deal. Since a Golden Dawn Temple is being instituted here and there throughout not only this country, but the world as a whole, this counsel might be very useful to all concerned to enhance the whole process of initiation.

Once this were accomplished, they could either go their own separate ways or maintain the relationship for mutual aid and comfort. But from there, with the aid of the Opening by Watchtower, as it has come to be called, the elemental initiations would be taken care of, and from there they face the task of the Adeptus Minor initiation. What needs to be done in that regard is something I would rather not speculate about. But as one initiate has said, all that remains is to prepare the Temple and then hope and pray that it may become indwelled.

This entire discussion however is intended to be suggestive only. A great deal must be left to the ingenium of the student involved in this great adventure. Their intuition must be sharpened by their adherence to the work itself, and their progress and their plans must left to unfold by itself. Enough has been said at least to show that the way is not without light, and however bleak the path seemed without teachers and a temple of the Order, they are not left to stumble unaided in the darkness of the outer world. For as the Ritual says "My soul wanders in darkness and I seek the Light of the hidden Knowledge".

In conclusion it is strongly suggested that student closely study two or three of the discussions in this present volume. One of them is the Cautionary Note which directly follows this. Another is a document dealing with the Inflation of the Ego, a result which is to be avoided at all costs by self observation and study. And finally the important article written by Hyatt and myself concerning some major errors and confusions which students have made in the past. Other documents scattered throughout the different segments of this book will also be found supremely helpful in achieving the ends desired.

A CAUTIONARY NOTE

During the period of time when most of this work was in the manuscript phase, and various typists were working on it, their occasional comments concerning the Golden Dawn System perturbed me somewhat. It was Christopher Hyatt one of the editors of Falcon Press who first alerted me to the possibility that this misunderstanding might occur, suggesting therefore that I interpolate a cautionary word to prevent other readers developing the same misconception.

He was absolutely right, for some of them, as well as one or two subsequent readers, seem to have developed the conception that the whole Golden Dawn System was based on the initiatory rituals, and nothing more. It puzzled me because I had labored under the delusion that the rituals themselves indicated without equivocation that there was far more to the system than the rituals themselves, and also because the remainder of the volume itself elaborated a whole system of magical practice which could exist altogether independently of the initiatory rituals.

I was so certain of this that to a couple of them I had confided that though for the time being my interest in writing was exhausted, nonetheless some time in the future I felt compelled to write yet another book establishing a relationship between Tibetan magical practices, as for example laid out in Evans Wentz's book *Milarepa the Tibetan Yogi* and the Golden Dawn System. There are innumerable parallels which are worth investigating and enumerating. And these are altogether apart from the matter of initiatory rituals. I feel strongly therefore that I must not proceed too far with this book without stressing the fact that there is infinitely more to the Golden Dawn System of Magic than the initiatory and other types of rituals. Not that I want to minimize the importance of their role in the entire system but it comprises so much more that it puzzled me how anyone could avoid the realization that the performance of the rituals satisfactorily depends on so much more. If the student has thoroughly studied the Z-1 and Z-3 documents, it should have dawned upon him that efficacy of any ritual depends entirely on all the participants having acquired considerable skills in the magical work prescribed by the Order.

Apart from the rudimentary art of invocation by means of the Pentagram and Hexagram, there is a vast repertory of techniques which must be used and mastered, not merely to gain advancement to a higher grade in the Order, which is not too terribly important by and of itself, but in order to become a proficient student of Magic these must be not merely known but wholly mastered. For example, assumption of God forms and the ability to build up Telesmatic Images, more or less along the same line, these two are the very foundations of practical theurgy. Then there is the Middle Pillar technique whose importance simply cannot be overemphasized in any way. The student who has neglected to achieve considerable proficiency in this particular practice will find himself frustrated at every turn. And finally there is the vibratory formula of the Middle Pillar. I cannot conceive of a ritual of any kind being successfully consummated without being adept in the use of the vibratory formula. I have elaborated this in a rather new way, I fancy, in that section dealing with this matter, and I urge the prospective student of magic to pay particular attention not only to this, but to all the techniques I have just mentioned.

Nor is the main thesis of the Order the memorization of dry Qabalistic knowledge from the Knowledge Lectures or from any other text for that matter. This material represents the dry bones of Order knowledge, the basic alphabet of what has come to be known as the Magical Language. Every science and every Art has its own language without which there can be little communication. A great deal of undergraduate university work consists mainly of learning different kinds of *languages* that belong to the various sciences one is learning about. For example, physics has its own terminology without which little headway can be made in mastering its complex mysteries. The same is true of geology which must forever remain a mystery to those who will not master its language. Even in the behavioral sciences a whole new jargon or language must be assimilated. Eventually many students learn to use the jargon so satisfactorily and skillfully that they become unintelligible in their everyday conversations leading their critics to condemn the jargon in which they have steeped themselves. Nonetheless, it is a language of its own. It must be learned, mastered and used in order to become an effective means of communication. Much the same is true of the magical language. It is a highly complex one, and most of this work lays down the elemental principles of this language. The student will do well to take this time mastering it–that is if he has never been exposed to it before. But when he does become familiar with this language, he will never fall into the booby trap that *The Complete Golden Dawn System of Magic* comprises this item or that item only. It is a vast and comprehensive system that is worthy of considerable effort to make it an integral part of one's thinking and feeling.

Finally of course there is the method of the tattwa vision, also called skrying in the spirit vision. This is most important. However I feel entirely too much attention in the past has been paid to this method at the expense of some of those just listed. There must have been many members of the early Order who had a great talent for skrying, since it led to the possible development of clairvoyance, etc. For this reason, its use was overdone. Not only was this so, but some of the protective methods were neglected, and some of the people became gullible and credulous, and lost their natural scepticism which is one of the indispensable factors absolutely essential to the welfare of the student of magic. Without it he is lost in a wilderness of deception and fantasy. Nothing solid can be based upon this whatsoever. Of course there are also the divinatory methods of the Order. Geomancy and the Tarot. But the student must not stop there. These methods appear to be devoted to divining the future, etc., but it would be a great mistake if your interpretations were limited solely to this. Apart from the fact that the use of these methods develop intuition and the inner psychospiritual senses, there is a whole inner world to be explored and discovered by using the geomantic symbols and the Tarot cards themselves as gateways to another dimension of existence, to another aspect of ourselves of which we ordinarily have little consciousness. And since the work of the Order is based upon self discovery as suggested by the injunction in the Neophyte Ritual "Quit the night and seek the Day," and by the very name of the Order itself–The Golden Dawn, a symbolic representation of the spiritual experience which is the goal of all our work, it is the attainment of the awareness of divinity, and then bringing this divinity to operate in our daily lives in this world of Malkuth which is the outer garment of God. I still like the old Qabalistic aphorism that Kether is in Malkuth, and Malkuth is in Kether but after another manner. This is not unrelated to the Mahayan aphorism that Nirvana is Samsara and Samsara is Nirvana.

Nor must I forget to call attention to something that is all too often neglected. Meditation on the significance and meaning of the magical instruments. They are often made and consecrated by members of the Order and used as always recommended, but rarely do they come to terms with what underlies their common usage. It should be obvious to any long term student that the Lotus Wand for example is a symbol, amongst others, of the spinal column with the Lotus at the top of the head–a channel for the movement of the spinal spirit fire, the Kundalini. (In this connection do make an effort to obtain and read a book by a Hindu named Gopi Krishna entitled *Kundalini*). All the other instruments similarly have profound meanings. In this connection, as an aid to meditation, I can strongly recommend Aleister Crowley's magnificent early book *Part Two of Book Four* dealing with the theory of Magick and its tools. There are some beautiful meditative descriptions of the elemental weapons which the good student cannot afford to overlook or do without. Since insights will grow as he grows, insight and intuition piling on one another until, of course, the ultimate goal of all the work is realized–enlightenment.

As one becomes proficient in the work of the Order and one's insight and understanding develops, it will become apparent that all of these methods may be tied together and unified to become a magical engine by means of which the Mountain of Initiation may be scaled and the Kingdom of Heaven reached, so that man aspires to God and God aspires to man.

The Order is a magical one. But its mysticism is by no means to be separated from its magic. At first they may seem to be entirely different methods of attaining to the highest. And indeed so they appear to be. But it is the mark of real adeptship when the student comes to realize that there is no real separation between these methods, and that at the end they are one and the same.

In other words, to come back to the initial theme stated at the outset of this chapter, there is much more to the Order than the initiatory and other types of rituals. There is so much in the Neophyte and Adeptus Minor rituals that are of value to the aspirant, that even if one were to assume that the Order work is essentially that of ritualism, one would really not be far wrong. They contain so much. For example in the Neophyte Ritual, one of the first exhortations one hears is that coming from the Hierophant who states by names and images are all power awakened and reawakened. The newly initiated Frater or Soror into the Order could spend considerable effort and time meditating on just what this means. When he does this, he will be led into the deepest mysteries of the teachings of the Order, and into some kind of understanding of what all the variety of Order techniques amount to. I can come to rest here about warning the student to dispense with any superficial evaluation of the Order method arrived at by a rapid reading of the several rituals, or of the book itself. The whole system needs to be studied carefully. Don't be misled by the apparent simplicity of the system. It is enormously complex and complicated–and at the same time so beautifully simple. It may take the student some time, perhaps years, to appreciate the simplicity of the Order system, but the expenditure of that time will be found to be worth the effort. Though meditation is not exactly harped on throughout the text, it is mentioned upon what he learns and does with the Order work. There is much to be gained. So much is not stated in specific words, but it is in this "non-statement" or understatement that much of the essence of the system is contained.

Just recently (Easter, 1983) another comment was made, one which I have heard before from one of the Order "failures," that there is a dearth of the devotional element in the Order work. Ordinarily, this comment might be expected from a former Church goer steeped in the Bible–or, which amounts to the same thing, a member of the Fellowship of the Rosy Cross, the name of the Waite version of the Golden Dawn.

Ordinarily, this criticism is not worthy of note, save that in the last instance when I heard it, a younger student had just returned from one of the Ashrams in India where he had heard a great deal about bhakta yoga. I can understand this criticism because bhakta is certainly not stressed in the overt sense within the Order work. But I have to remind students that if they study the Order work very closely–as closely as they have been taught to study the yoga system, they will discover a great deal of emotional content. For instance, on the few occasions when I have witnessed a Neophyte initiation, I have felt very close to an emotional exaltation, almost enough to bring on tears or at the very least of sense of choking, adequate to halt speech. Moreover, the Hierophant of one of the existent Temples, V.H. Soror S.I.A.A., who has officiated at the initiation of some forty Neophytes, also tells me that the ceremony often brings her to the verge of tears.

Apart from that, however, I strongly urge the student who may entertain similar feelings, to read once more a former work of mine *What You Should Know About the Golden Dawn*, (Falcon Press, Phoenix, AZ. 1983). In that book, many quotations from the different rituals are given, quotations which are one only choice

English and fine writing, but are good examples of the devotional aspect of the Order's work. These are really worth reviewing quite often so as to renew the sense that the Order is not without its bhakta aspects.

If that is not enough, then I must refer to the work of Aleister Crowley who, after all, whatever is said and done, was once a member of the Order and owes a very great deal to his Initiation therein. I especially suggest reading his instruction which reviews the whole Eastern attitude about bhakti–*Liber Asarte vel Berylli* to be found in one of the Equinoxes, or in my book *Gems from the Equinox* (Falcon Press, Phoenix, AZ. 1982). So far as I am concerned, this *Liber* is a masterpiece, which I can strongly recommend especially to one complaining of the absence of devotional writing in the Order.

Furthermore, and this I think is paramount, there is Crowley's early masterpiece *Three Holy Books* originally published by Sangreal Foundation with a short introduction by me, but which I understand will be republished by Samuel Weiser Inc. of New York. This volume contains *Liber LXV* or *The Book of the Heart Girt with a Serpent*, *Liber VII* or *Liber Lapidis Lazuli*, and finally *Liber 813 vel Ararita*. All three are superbly written and breathe devotion in every word. I am particularly fond of *LXV* and *VII* which Falcon Press is issuing as cassettes, containing *Liber LXV*, or T*he Book of the Heart Girt with a Serpent, Liber VII* or *Liber Lapidus Lazuli*, and *Liber DCCCXIII* or Ararita. Periodically I will play the tape on retiring to bed at night, and permitting myself to fall asleep listening to its beauty and devotion. It may be stretching definitions of things pretty far to state that these may be considered these to be in that category than the religious lucubrations of Mr. A. E. Waite who was also once a member of the Order. He founded his own Fellowship, and rewrote the

Rituals (three of which are included in a later section of this book) to include excerpts from the Bible and perhaps from the Roman missal. I am not to be construed as being antagonistic to the latter by any means, but I do state strongly that if I must use one or the other, I prefer to use the so-called holy books of Aleister Crowley. They convey more devotion and love to me than almost anything else. So that if there is actually a dearth of devotional material in the Rituals and work of the Order, it is more than compensated for by reference to the work of a former member, Aleister Crowley. I trust that this will be the end of any complaints about his topic.

THE PROPER ATTITUDE TOWARD MIND-BODY

Over the past fifty years I have insisted that the serious magical student seek a course of therapy as a safeguard against some of the catastrophic results which appear to overtake too many of our promising students.

The difficulties seem to arise from the following:

THE SUPEREGO AND THE H.G.A.

A. The confusion between the Freudian superego (the unconscious infantile conscience) and the Order's concept of the Higher and Divine Genius (or the H.G.A.)

Many students as well as those not involved with Magic often substitute a form of their infantile conscience for one form of "Higher Self" or another. This can lead to nothing but disaster. Instead of being guided by a Higher Genius the person is really at the mercy of infantile "voices" and values, so-called brain chatter. Not only does this cause undue individual suffering and deception, it also causes a complete halt to any real progress in the Theurgic arts and sciences. To a large extent his confusion contributes to the often "bad" reputation students of the occult possess.

Those of you familiar with the history of the Order can find glowing examples of this folly. However there is no need to delve this deeply. Almost any group or Order has members and often leaders who have fallen head long into this pit dug for he unwary.

THE INFLATION OF THE EGO

B. There is a frightening frequency of the occurrence of the inflation of the ego–sometimes referred to as infantile megalomania. To help the student understand this difficulty let us define the healthy ego as a computer type decision maker. The ego's function is to help the person make decisions based on hard data. The purpose of this function should be that of survival and personal fulfillment on various levels or planes. In one sense the healthy ego is more or less non-personal. It realizes cause and effect in Malkuth, and understands its limitations.

On the other hand infantile megalomania is a natural occurrence in infancy, and with proper development has been outgrowth by the healthy adult ego. However, while this is the ideal it rarely occurs in practice, and requires some form of "therapy" Eastern or Western to accomplish this goal. In the practice of Magic or anything which release unusual amounts of energy from the unconscious the infantile megalomaniacal substructure is re-activated, and all the illusions and delusions of self importance and elevation of babyhood re-emerge. This flattery overwhelms the ego. The person takes the impersonal and universal nature of the powers he or she experiences as if he or she created the powers or experiences by what they call - *themselves*.

If this experience called by Jung the "Mana Personality" persists for too long a period the person becomes ego-maniacal and thoroughly self-centered. This can be observed in patients undergoing psychotherapy as well as in the so-called normal man on the street. This excessive self-admiration or as Jung puts it "the naive concretization of primordial images" leads to an overinflated ego which in the end leads directly to disaster and contradicts in toto the purpose of the Great Work.

The student should be also cautioned that the opposite of infantile megalomania is not milk-toast humility and passiveness. The latter is the sine qua non of a deeply buried and potentially more dangerous form of infantile megalomania.

THE PROPER ATTITUDE TOWARD THE INSTINCTS

C. There is a danger of the blatant acting out of instincts which have been distorted through repression and denial on the one hand or their compulsive repression leading to a boring and unfulfilled sex life. Almost everyone raised in the current Judaic-Christian morality suffers inevitably from a totally distorted attitude towards this topic as well as to all biological functions in general. Therefore a complete sex life which is not only pleasurable but aids in the evolution of the Soul is totally out of the question. What is required is a healthy attitude toward all bodily functions, remembering always that Kether is in Malkuth and Malkuth is in Kether, but after another manner.

Those involved with the Great Work have often found themselves falling into the camps of excess in one direction or another, i.e. too much or too little. The proper use and enjoyment of sex is a necessary part in the discovery and development of the Higher Genius. Aleister Crowley is one of very few who has recognized the reality of this problem, although he himself at times, due to his Plymouth Brethren upbringing, fell into the same booby trap. Most of us are plagued by an average somewhat inhibited sex life, or worse yet a compulsive acting out of our repressed sexual drives. These attitudes do not aid the development of self-expression, deep and total relaxation, or serve as a vehicle for opening the deeper channels which lie within.

THE PROBLEM OF RELIGION AND THE GREAT WORK

This opens the way to a discussion of a very serious point which has long been on my mind. It emerges into the open by the inclusion in this volume of some of the Rituals of A.E. Waite. **Mathers and the Order he founded were only nominally Christian.** One has to search meticulously through the Rituals and other teaching for serious literal interpretations of the historical Jesus. In reality they are absent. The references to Osiris as a symbol of man-made-perfect could be those of any of the mythical Mediterranean crucified Gods, of whom there were many. The Order was a Hermetic Brotherhood and Christianity played only a minimal role in its operation. Mathers was on a friendly basis with Anna Kingford who had founded another Hermetic Society in which Christianity did play a prominent part. But he never permitted this friendship to influence him to make his Society similar to hers.

There is a very interesting set of concepts here that need only to be touched on. And that is the constant effort made by some occult teachers to Christianize the ancient wisdom religion. I have already mentioned Anna Kingsford as one. Another, who influenced Dr. Felkins tremendously was Rudolph Steiner who seemed determined to Christianize occultism in grotesque ways that are fundamentally opposed to the innate conceptual nature of Magic. In this he was following in the foot steps of Annie Besant and Bishop Leadbeater who had already succeeded in corrupting Blavatskian Theosophy, transforming it into a Christian occultism with Easter overtones. Though Steiner was in conflict with them, nonetheless their doctrines must have affected him profoundly, despite his so-called clairvoyance being in opposition to the so-called clairvoyance of Leadbeater.

While this was going on Waite who had been raised as a Roman Catholic seemed determined to follow in the footsteps of the above named teachers. After the revolt of 1900 in the Order he was one of the several committee members who ran the Order. Later he pulled out from this committee to form his own Fellowship of The Rosy Cross. When this happened he totally revised not merely the rituals of the Order but the entire philosophic context of the Order. In this volume three of his Rituals are included. From them the discriminating reader will be able to determine to what extent this perversion of the Order methodology had advanced. There is almost no relationship between the teachings originally laid down and the later biblical emphasis introduced by Waite.

This of course resulted in the introduction of Church concepts of morality and purity which are evident in almost everything that Waite wrote. His whole attitude became sex-negative as well as occult-negative. He made it almost a point of honour to eradicate any reference to every item in the Magical curriculum laid down by Mathers and Westcott. Fortunately when he died in the late 1930s his Order died with him and so did his sex-negative attitudes, as well as his wretched pompous English–characterized by a need to use Latin phrases where simple English would have been much better. Contrary to the common point of view he must have been a very ambitious person and this is made evident by the pompous titles he gave both to himself in the Rituals as well as to his attendant officers.

EGOTISM

One of the great dangers inherent within the practice of Magic and indeed of all the occult arts–is the development of an enormous egotism characterized by messianic feelings, infantile omnipotence and the utter destruction of any capacity for effective self-criticism. It appears that as the student becomes more adept in the skills of meditation, skrying, or ceremonial work, he becomes more threatened by an inflation of the ego. It appears slowly and insidiously, without apparent warning. Only those people who are closely related to or associated with the student become aware of the subtle metamorphosis that occurs. The student rarely is conscious of this unconscious transformation. Attempting to make him aware of this egotism is doomed to failure; it is like knocking on a stone wall.

It seems to afflict the aspirant who functions outside the borders of an occult order or legitimate magical school. In this sense, most students come within the jurisdiction of this definition. Those who practice their occult work under the aegis of a legitimate magical body or under the guidance of an experienced and wise guru or teacher seem to be more protected from this inflation–unless the guru has himself fallen under the spell of his own messianic fantasies and inflation. If he has, then he communicates his fatal sickness to his students. Or else he is wholly blinded to the debacle about to occur to his student.

One has only to look at the history of most modern occultists and I use them preferentially because their history is more readily authenticated than those of earlier times–to perceive how valid this phenomenon is. So many of them developed fantastic notions of their own unique importance and role in the world or even cosmic picture. Only recently I heard of one who claimed to have been the teacher of Jesus? There are an almost infinite number of variations of this theme.

It is a definite and ever present danger, and all students of occultism within or without occult orders must become conscious of this phenomenon. Otherwise they are doomed. They experience what appears to be at first an enhancement of life-feelings, a rich harvest of previously unknown information and knowledge, and the awareness that destiny has suddenly acquired a new direction,– only to collapse later in total frustration, ignominy, and exile from all of society.

From the theoretical viewpoint, the gradual expansion of the confines of the limited ego by magical practices, leads to contact of some kind with the 'unconscious'. A new source of energy is released, an energy which is seen as carrying with it not only new feelings but new knowledge and a greater capacity for self-confidence with the ability to impress and motive one's fellow man. This energy floods the unprepared ego with almost infinite promise. Unless the candidate is properly prepared for this phenomenon, or is guided and guarded by a competent experience teacher, he is likely to take this seriously. Effective self-criticism seems to have vanished in thin air.

Crowley seems to have been most conscious of this in some of his earlier work. He himself had a couple of admirable teachers– Alan Bennett, George Cecil Jones and Oscar Eckenstein. For example in one section of *Liber O* he wrote: 'This book is very easy to misunderstand: readers are asked to use the most minute critical care in the study of it, even as we have done in its preparation. In this book it is spoken of the Sephiroth and the Paths; of Spirits and Conjurations; of Gods, Spheres, Planes and many other things which may or may not exist. It is immaterial whether these exist or not. **By doing certain things certain results will follow; students are most earnestly warned against attributing objective reality or philosophic validity to any of them.** There is little danger that any student, however idle or stupid, will fail to get some result; but there is great danger that he will be led astray, obsessed and overwhelmed by his results, even though it be by those which it is necessary that he should attain. Too often, moreover, he mistaketh the final resting-place for the goal, and taketh off his armour as if he were a victor ere the fight is well begun.'

Some few other occultists familiar with the practical side of things also utter similar warnings. Blavatsky in her *Voice of the Silence* also warns that 'under every flower a serpent coiled.' And in a footnote in this warning, she adds: 'The astral region, the psychic world of supersensuous perception and of deceptive sights–the world of mediums. It is the great 'Astral Serpent' of Eliphas Levi. No blossom picked in those regions has ever yet been brought down to earth without its serpent coiled around the stem. It is the world of the **Great Illusion**.'

Only a good guru of almost superhuman powers of effective self-evaluation and examination provide the means of avoiding inflation and the consequent disaster. A third means is almost any form of good psychotherapy. The latter appears to be able to drain off the massive uncontrolled quantities of energy that are released and direct them into new and constructive goals. Those Reichians who have an understanding of 'occult' matters would appear to be more effective than most in dealing with the phenomenon.

Jung has also described it most extensively in an extraordinary good essay in a book entitled *Two Essays on Analytical Psychology*. However, the methods of therapy described by Jung and practised by his followers leave a lot to be desired. Every occult student should not merely read this book but own it, in order to provide the opportunity to read and re-read many times the chapter dealing with inflation of the ego.

It is his contention that the analysand, the patient undergoing therapy–analogous to the enterprising student beginning his occult work–attempts to identify his ego with the collective psyche. He does this as a means of escaping the pain and anxiety resulting from the collapse of his conscious persona or self, which is one of the primary effects of the analysis. To free himself from the seductive embrace of the collective psyche, instead of denying it as some others have done, he accepts it so totally that he is devoured or overwhelmed by it, becomes lost in it, and thus is no longer capable of perceiving it as a separate entity. As another student once put it, instead of realizing that they have become illuminated by God, they affirm that they *are* God. Thus the inflation begins. It ends disastrously when or if the 'God' discovers he is not omniscient or omnipotent. But by then it is generally too late.

It would not do the student harm to re-read the statement by Hyatt and myself on the problems confronting the serious occult student in the beginning of this book. Also while at times outrageous Hyatt's book *Undoing Yourself with Energized Meditation* (Falcon Press, 1982), makes good sense in this context.

INTRODUCTIONS
by Israel Regardie

The World's Tragedy
By Aleister Crowley - Copyright 1985 First Falcon Press Edition

INTRODUCTION
By Israel Regardie

Before proceeding with what needs to be said about this book by Aleister Crowley, acknowledgment must first be given to the University of Texas and to Dr. Decherd Turner, Director of its Humanities Research Center, for their kind response to my request for a copy of *The World's Tragedy*. Their xeroxed copy is deeply appreciated.

John Symonds, perhaps the most malicious of biographers of famous writers, once wrote that Crowley was not a particularly good poet. Maybe! I am offering to the general public this reprint of the 1910 Paris edition of *The World's Tragedy* so that they may judge whether Symonds knew what he was talking about. For Symonds' criticisms, let me add here–I have the most profound contempt; I have expressed this at much greater and more detailed length elsewhere (See my *Legend Of Aleister Crowley*, Falcon Press, 1983).

One of the first things that Crowley set me to do after I arrived in Paris to be his secretary in the year 1928. He took the original and first carbon, and I kept the second carbon copy. This is cherished and preserved for many long years until my house in Los Angeles was broken into by some unknown zealot who selectively stole all my Crowley first editions, amongst other valuable items, including the carbon copy of this book referred to above. I missed it badly, and despite twenty years of persistent search no other copy came my way.

Then, through various grapevines, I heard that the University of Texas had a splendid collection of Crowleyana. Upon request some years ago, a bibliography of that collection was sent me. Lo and behold! They had several copies of *The World's Tragedy*. Apparently my recent request for a xerox copy was honored upon learning that I felt strongly about all the writings of Aleister Crowley, believing that no one piece written by him, regardless of its nature, should be permitted to varnish from public scrutiny or to remain locked up in a university library. Thus they really have done mankind a great service.

The long, almost epic poem/play is one of the most bitter and vicious diatribes against Christianity that I have ever read. Especially the preface written by Crowley also. Throughout the years, whenever I contemplated the possibility of finding a copy and re-issuing this book, it occurred to me to omit altogether the preface since biographies of Crowley were now readily available. There was no need to duplicate history. There is Crowley's own autobiography *The Confessions* which he humorously called his Autohagiography. In addition there is my own *Eye In The Triangle*, (Falcon Press, 1982) which was really an answer to Symonds' wretched vilification of Crowley. It succeeded in dragging me out of a decade of literary silence and unproductivity. Susan Roberts' excellent biography *The Magician Of The Golden Dawn* must also be mentioned. (It must not be confused with Ellic Howe's hatchet job *The Magicians Of The Golden Dawn* which I reviewed critically in *Gnostica* some years ago.) These aforementioned three, apart from some few minor others, state clearly and emphatically what Crowley was about.

But when, upon receipt of the Xerox copy from Texas, I reread the Preface by Crowley, the realization dawned on me that this was not under any circumstances to be omitted. It was too powerful an indictment and historical denunciation, written in his own life blood, virulently expressing his deep and abiding hatred of Christianity–from which he never really recovered. The virus was too deeply embedded in his system, no matter how valiantly he rebelled and fought against it. The hatred was too often repeated and re-emphasized not to leave any doubt that its seeds were still actively infecting him.

Perhaps the most illuminating way of regarding this is in terms of Wilhelm Reich's concept of the character armor. Basically this comprises at least two elements–the psychic armor which for convenience sake may be compared with the Freudian superego, and the muscular armor which is the sum total of all the bodily tensions of the organism. The function of the armor–whether on the psychic level or muscular level–is to repress impulses and feelings that are not morally acceptable in terms of cultural-environmental attitudes and early family training. It is also worth reflecting that this functions both on the conscious and unconscious levels. One represses with one's body as much as with one's mind.

The armor has its origins in the earliest days, even moments of childhood, babyhood and gestation. It represents the firm hand of one or more parents, or those who stand in loco parentis, who uttered the first "no" or "don't" with or without other means of emphasis. Armor is the result of using fear and terror tactics to mold infants into "proper" replications of the cultural ethos. When it becomes fully developed, it functions autonomously and absolutely, in much the same way that the initial trainers did, demanding absolute obedience. So that the repressed material has not a chance in the world to emerge; it becomes wholly incorporated into the warp and woof of the armor. (See my book,

Reich—His Theory and Method, Falcon Press). If the repressed material appears at all it can only be in some modified or distorted form that bears apparently little relationship to its original nature.

It might be worthwhile for the student of Crowley to study further Wilhelm Reich's *Function Of The Orgasm* in order to gain better familiarity with these notions. They will help assuredly in an enhanced understanding of Crowley and especially of this Preface to *The World's Tragedy*.

His hatred of Christianity was not a blind unreasoned prejudicial emotion. It was indelibly rooted in his own personal experience, amplified and added to by extensive study and research all throughout his adult years. The basic cause of this undying hatred revolved around the Plymouth Brethren sect founded upon and dedicated to Biblical literalism. It was the religion of his boyhood, his parents having gone to fanatical extremes to ensure that he was a "good" Christian.

His total unmitigated hatred of Christianity is therefore no mystery. It becomes intelligible to the point where anyone with some sensitivity and compassion can have much sympathy with his point of view. All that is required is to gain some familiarity with the historical antecedents of his attitude.

His family as I have said were members of this Plymouth Brethren sect. It was a religious group that developed antagonism to the Church of England and so split off, having as the main stem of their faith biblical literalism. This was their rock, and this their guide-line through the stormy seas of life. No matter how attention might be called to the innumerable contradictions of one segment of the Bible as compared with another, these people developed a profound interpretative skill enabling them to justify and rationalize their behavior and whims at any one moment in terms of a specific chapter and verse.

The home situation presented insoluble conflicts to this boy. His father, previously a Quaker, was a devout member of this sect.

He loved to challenge people wherever they happened to be on basic questions of faith and their role in life. His mother was equally fanatical, though less well-informed. She played a dominant role in the development of whatever his character came to be, and in one form or another entered symbolically into all his mystical writing. He lived at first in a spiritual, social and intellectual vacuum. It left its distorting mark on him throughout his life.

All of this described in great detail and emotion in the Preface to this book. I trust the reader will remember it forever.

The anathema that he heaped on the schoolmaster of the Plymouth Brethren school that he had to attend, is a masterpiece of invective. It is easy to imagine him almost like one of the old Biblical prophets, coming down from the mountain, and in high dudgeon and indignation, cursing the people before him. Crowley was bred on the Bible. It was practically the only book that he was permitted to read. Its language became part and parcel of the structure of his mind. It is no wonder then that his curse has all the hallmarks of the Bible, so vitriolic and damning is in its entirety. He wrote:

"May God bite into the bones of men the pain of that hell on earth (I have prayed often) that by them it may be sowed with salt, accursed for ever! May the maiden that passes it be barren, and the pregnant woman that beholdeth it abort! May the birds of the air refuse to fly over it! May the wicked dwell therein! May the light of the Sun be with-held therefrom, and the light of the Moon not lighten it! May it become the home of the shells of the dead, and may the demons of the pit inhabit it! May it be accursed, accursed, accursed–accursed for ever and ever!

And still, standing as I stand in the prime of early manhood, free from all the fretters of the body and the mind, do I curse the memory thereof unto the ages."

The short section on sodomy is about the clearest confession of his own homosexuality that I have seen issue from his pen. The

Bagh-i-Muattar was written, I believe, somewhat later. While this is not my cup of tea, nevertheless each man has the right to find his own way through the sexual morass that surround this subject in our day. That was his way.

Yet he was not altogether homosexual. Whatever meanings may attach to the term bisexuality or to Freud's clumsy but felicitous phrase "polymorphous sexual perversions of childhood," these apply without question to him (See Norman O. Brown's shattering criticism of Freud's phrase in a book Crowley would have loved *Life Against Death*.)

That was his business, however. Nonetheless, the hatred of Christianity was not entirely his personal business. It is shared especially today by multitudes of thinking men and women. And though it may appear on the surface that Fundamentalism and Evangelism and Charismatic Christianity are spreading (even the previous President of the U.S. was numbered among their ranks), nevertheless it is the belief of many that these are the agonizing death rattles of a moribund and decadent religion. If so, Crowley's writing had a lot to do with that. He was unceasing in his eloquent denunciation of the religion that spoiled his early life and with hate and guilt ruined the lives of the untold legions of human beings. Most of those who practice any form of psychotherapy will corroborate this statement readily.

One of the major characteristics of Crowley as a person was his magnificent sense of humor which bubbled and overflowed almost without cessation. For the newcomer to his manifold literary output this humor was slightly disconcerting. Even in the midst of a colloquy on philosophy or religion or mysticism a joke or two, sometimes thoroughly ribald, would disrupt the continuity of his theme. It led some critics to believe that he was merely a jokester and therefore not to be taken seriously. Never was a greater mistake made.

In this book, the dramatic personae is hysterical by itself. Jehovah, the testy old senior of the Old Testament, is depicted as a mangy old Vulture named Yaugh Waugh. And his only begotten son "the lamb that taketh away the sins of the world," is depicted simply as the Lamb. The Holy Ghost, pictorialized by the descent of the dove, is engaged with Yaugh Waugh in machinations and plottings that do not please the Lamb in any way, and is simply named Pigeon. Their appearances on stage as it were intersperse the activities of handsome Greek lads and lasses who seem to be enjoying themselves in the dells and groves of the woodlands, quite unaware of the machinations of the unholy Three.

Let me close this short Introduction with the firm conviction that the book needs no defense. It stands on its own artistic and iconoclastic merit, which is considerable. And I must add that it gives me enormous pleasure and profound satisfaction to know that I have had a part in giving back to the world a document that is as important in its own way as the Bill of Rights is to Americans.

Israel Regardie
Arizona, 1983

The Golden Dawn
Copyright 1937 - 1982 Llewellyn Publications

INTRODUCTION
By Israel Regardie

It was in the year 1890 that Dr. Franz Hartmann, in an endeavour to provide a simple outline of the vicissitudes of what came to be known as the Rosicrucian Order, wrote a book entitled *In the Pronaos of the Temple*. The central figure of this history was a monk Fr. R. C.–described in the earliest Rosicrucian manifesto the *Fama Fraternitatis* as the "pious, spiritual and highly-illuminated Father...It is said that he was a German nobleman who had been educated in a convent, and that long before the time of the Reformation he had made a pilgrimage to the Holy Land in company with another brother of this convent, and that while at Damascus they had been initiated by some learned Arabs into the mysteries of the secret science. After remaining three years at Damascus, they went to Fez, in Africa, and there they obtained still more knowledge of magic, and of the relations existing between the macrocosm and microcosm. After having also travelled in Spain, he returned to Germany, where he founded a kind of convent called *Sanctus Spiritus*, and remaining there writing his secret science and continuing his studies. He then accepted as his assistants, at first, three, and afterwards, four more monks from the same convent in which he had been educated, and thus founded the first society of the Rosicrucians. They then laid down the results of their science in books, which are said to be still in existence, and in the hands of some Rosicrucians. It is then said that 120 years after his death, the entrance to his tomb was discovered. A stair-case led into a subterranean vault, at the door of which was written, *Post annos CXX patebo*. There was a light burning in the vault, which, however, became extinct as soon as it was approached. The vault had seven sides and seven angles, each side being five feet wide and eight feet high. The upper part represented the firmament, the floor, the earth, and they were laid out in triangles, while each side was divided into ten squares. In the middle was an altar, bearing a brass plate, upon which were engraved the letters, A.C. R.C., and the words *Hoc Universi Compendium vivus mihi Sepulchrum feci*. In the midst were four figures surrounded by the words, *Nequaquam Vacuum. Legis Jugum. Libertas Evangelii. Dei Gloria Intacta*. Below the altar was found the body of *Rosenkreutz*, intact, and without any signs of putrefaction. In his hand was a book of parchment, with golden letters marked on the cover with a T, and at the end was written, *Ex Deo nascimur. In Jesus morimur. Per Spiritum Sanctum reviviscimus*."

It was upon this schema and from this original body, to state it briefly, that the Hermetic Order of the Golden Dawn claimed direct descent. Its history lecture, however, volunteered very few verifiable details as to the historical facts which, from the scholarly point of view, we should be acquainted with–the details for example of the line of descent from, say, 1614 to 1865. Current within the present day Order was the belief that at various dates within the period named, the Order as an organised body of students ceased to exist. Instead, there was an oral continuation of teaching from isolated initiates here, there and everywhere, until more recent times when religious and political conditions did not militate against the advisability of formulating a group. With the institution of a definite body, the original system of grades was re-established, and the systems of Alchemy, the Qabalah and Magic once more were taught to zealous, aspiring Neophytes. As a cloak to their activities, they likewise continued in the early agreement of the Order which was:

"*First*, that none of them should profess any other thing than to cure the sick, and that gratis.

Second, None of the posterity should be constrained to wear one certain kind of habit, but therein to follow the custom of the country.

Third, that every year, upon the day C. they should meet together at the house Sanctus Spiritus, or write the cause of his absence.

Fourth, Every Brother should look about for a worthy person who, after his decease, might succeed him.

Fifth, The word R. C. should be their seal, mark, and character.

Sixth, The Fraternity should remain secret one hundred years.

With this preliminary account, we may turn to the claims of the Order within the more historical times of the late 19th century, though unfortunately, these claims are no more verifiable and certainly no clearer than those which charactised its beginning.

"The Order of the Golden Dawn," narrates the history lecture of that Order, "is an Hermetic Society whose members are taught the principles of Occult Science and the Magic of Hermes. During the early part of the second half of last century, several eminent Adepti and Chiefs of the Order in France and England died, and their death caused a temporary dormant condition of Temple work.

"Prominent among the Adepti of our Order and of public renown were Eliphas Levi the greatest of modern French magi; Ragon, the author of several books of occult lore; Kenneth M. Mackenzie, author of the famous and learned Masonic Encyclopaedia; and Frederick Hockley possessed of the power of vision in the crystal, and whose manuscripts are highly esteemed. These and other contemporary Adepti of this Order received their knowledge and power from predecessors of equal and even of greater and even of greater eminence. They received indeed and have handed down to us their doctrine and system of Theosophy and Hermetic Science and the higher Alchemy from a long series of practised investigators whose origin is traced to the Fratres Roseae Crucis of Germany, which association was founded by one Christian Rosenkreutz about the year 1398 A.D.

"The Rosicrucian revival of Mysticism was but a new development of the vastly older wisdom of the Qabalistic Rabbis and of that very ancient secret knowledge, the Magic of the Egyptians, in which the Hebrew Pentateuch tells you that Moses, the founder of the Jewish system was 'learned', that is, in which he had been initiated."

In a slender but highly informative booklet entitled Data of the History of the Rosicrucians published in 1916 by the late Dr. William Wynn Westcott, we find the following brief statement: "In 1887 by permission of S.D.A. a continental Rosicrucian Adept, the Isis-Urania Temple of Hermetic Students of the G.D. was formed to give instruction in the mediaeval Occult sciences. Fratres M.E.V. with S.A. and S.R.M.D. became the chiefs, and the latter wrote the rituals in modern English from old Rosicrucian mss. (the property of S.A.) supplemented by his own literary researches."

In these two statements is narrated the beginning of the Hermetic Order of the Golden Dawn–an organisation which has exerted a greater influence on the development of Occultism since its revival in the last quarter of the 19th century than most people can reliase. There can be little or no doubt that the Golden Dawn is, or rather was until very recently, the sole depository of magical knowledge, the only Occult Order of any real worth that the West in our time has known. A great many other occult organisations owe what little magical knowledge is theirs to leakages issuing from that Order and from its renegade members.

The membership of the Golden Dawn was recruited from every circle, and it was represented by dignified professions as well as by all the arts and sciences, to make but little mention of the trades and business occupations. It included physicians, psychologists, clergymen, artists and philosophers. And normal men and women, humble and unknown, from every walk of life have drawn inspiration from its font of wisdom, and undoubtedly many would be happy to recognise and admit the enormous debt they owe to it.

As an organisation, it preferred after the fashion of its mysterious parent always to shroud itself in an impenetrable cloak of mystery. Its teaching and methods of instruction were stringently guarded by serious penalties attached to the most awe-inspiring obligations in order to ensure that secrecy. So well have these obligations, with but one or two exceptions, been kept that the general public knows next to nothing about the Order, its teaching, or the extent and nature of its membership. Though this book will touch upon the teaching of the Golden Dawn, concerning its membership as a whole the writer will have nothing to say, except perhaps to repeat what may already to be more or less well-known. For instance, it is common knowledge that W. B. Yeats, Arthur Machen and, if rumour may be trusted, the late Arnold Bennett were at one time among its members, together with a good many other writers and artists.

With regard to the names given in Dr. Westcott's statement it is necessary that we bestow to them some little attention in order to unravel, so far as may be possible, the almost inextricable confusion which has characterised every previous effort to detail the history of the Order M.E.V. was the motto chosen by Dr. William Robert

Woodman, an eminent Freemason of the last century. Sapere Aude and Non Omnis Moriar were the two mottoes used by Dr. Westcott, an antiquarian, scholar, and coroner by profession. S.R.M.D. or S. Rhiogail Ma Dhream was the motto of S.L. MacGregor Mathers, the translator of *The Greater Key of King Solomon*, the *Book of the Sacred Magic of Abramelin the Mage*, and *The Kabbalah Unveiled*, which latter consisted of certain portions of the Zohar prefixed by an introduction of high erudition. He also employed the Latin motto Deo Duce Comite Ferro. S.D.A. was the abbreviation of the motto Sapiens Dominabitur Astris chosen by a Fraulein Anna Sprengel of Nuremburg, Germany. Such were the actors on this occult stage, this the *dramatis personae* in the background of the commencement of the Order. More than any figures who may later have prominently figured in its government and work, these are the four outstanding figures publicly involved in the English foundation of what came to be known as The Hermetic Order of the Golden Dawn.

How the actual instigation of the Order came to pass is not really known. Or rather, because of so many conflicting stories and legends the truth is impossible to discover. At any rate, so far as England is concerned, without a doubt we must seek for its origin in the Societas Rosicruciana in Anglia. This was an organisation formulated in 1865 by eminent Freemasons, some of them claiming authentic Rosicrucian initiation from continental authorities. Amongst those who claimed such initiation was one Kenneth H. Mackenzie, a Masonic scholar and encyclopaedist, who had received his at the hands of a Count Apponyi in Austria. The objects of this Society which confined its membership to Freemasons in good standing, was "to afford mutual aid and encouragement in working out the great problems of Life, and in discovering the secrets of naturel to facilitate the study of the systems of philosophy founded upon the Kaballah and the doctrines of Hermes Trismegistus." Dr. Westcott also remarks that today its Fratres "are concerned in the study and administration of medicines, and in their manufacture upon old lines; they also teach and practise the curative effects of coloured light, and cultivate mental processes which are believed to induce spiritual enlightenment and extended powers of the human senses, especially in the directions of clairvoyance and clairaudience."

The first Chief of this Society, its Supreme Magus so-called, was one Robert Wentworth Little who is said to have rescued some old rituals from a certain Masonic storeroom, and it was from certain of those papers that the Society's rituals were elaborated. He died in 1878, and in his stead was appointed Dr. William R. Woodman. Both Dr. Westcott and MacGregor Mathers were prominent and active members of this body. In fact, the former became Supreme Magus upon Woodman's death, the office of Junior Magus being conferred upon Mathers. One legend has it that one day Westcott discovered in his library a series of cipher manuscripts, and in order to decipher them he enlisted the aid of MacGregor Mathers. It is said that this library was that of the Societas Rosicruciana in Anglia, and it is likewise asserted that those cipher manuscripts were among the rituals and documents originally rescued by Robert Little from Freemason's Hall. Yet other accounts have it that Westcott or a clerical friend found the manuscripts on a bookstall in Farringdon Street. Further apocryphal legends claim that they were found in the library of books and manuscripts inherited from the mystic and clairvoyant, Frederick Hockly who died in 1885. Whatever the real origin of these mysterious cipher manuscripts, when eventually deciphered with the aid of MacGregor Mathers, they were alleged to have contained the address of a Fraulin Anna Sprengel who purported to be a Rosicrucian Adept, in Nuremburg. Here was a discovery which, naturally, not for one moment was neglected. Its direct result was a lengthy correspondence with

Fraulein Sprengel, culminating in the transmission of authority to Woodman, Westcott and Mathers, to formulated in England a semi-public occult organisation which was to employ an elaborate an elaborate magical ceremonial, Qabalistlic teaching, and a comprehensive scheme of spiritual training, and a comprehensive scheme of spiritual training. Its foundation was designed to include both men and women on a basis of perfect equality in contradiction to the policy of the Societas Rosicruciana in Anglia which was comprised wholly of Freemasons. Thus, in 1887, the Hermetic Order of the Golden Dawn was established. Its first English Temple, Isis-Urania, was opened in the following year.

There is a somewhat different version as to its origin, having behind it the authority of Frater F.R., the late Dr. Felkin, who was the Chief of the Stella Matutina as well as a member of the Societas Rosicruciana. According to his account, and the following words, are substantially his own, prior to 1880 members of the Rosicrucian Order on the Continent selected with great care their own candidates whom they thought suitable for personal instruction. For these pupils they were each individually responsible, the pupils they were each individually responsible, the pupils thus selected being trained by them in the theoretical traditional knowledge now used in the Outer Order. After some three or more years of intensive private study these pupils were presented to the Chiefs of the Order, and if approved and passed by examination, they then received their initiation into the Order of the Roseae Rubeae et Aureae Crucis.

The political state of Europe in the nineteenth century was such that the strictest secrecy as to the activities of these people was very necessary. England, however, where many Masonic bodies and semi-private organisations were flourishing without interference, was recognised as having far greater freedom and liberty than the countries in which the continental Adepts were domiciled. Some, but by no means all, suggested therefore that in England open Temple work might be inauguraged. And Dr. Felkin here adds, though without the least word of explanation as to what machinery was set in motion of explanation as to what machinery was set in motion towards the attainment of that end, "and so it was...It came about then that Temples, arose in London, Bradford, Weston-super-Mare, and Edinburgh. The ceremonies we have were elaborated from cipher manuscripts, and all went well for a time."

Since the history of the Hermetic Order of the Golden Dawn subsequent to this period has already been narrated elsewhere there is little need to repeat it. Those who may be interested in a detailed meticulous history of the Rosicrucian claim as it has existed in Europe during the past three hundred years are advised to consult Arthur Edward Waite's *The Brotherhood of the Rosy Cross*. While in my small work *My Rosicrucian Adventure* the events that occurred to the Golden Dawn, culminating in this present publication of its teaching and rituals, are delineated at some length. The motives which have confirmed me in this decision to act contrary to the obligation of secrecy are there presented and discussed. And with these directions, let us pass from historical bones to what is the dynamic life and soul of the Order, its teaching and ceremonial technique of initiation.

Before one can grasp the nature of ceremonial initiation, which was the assumed function of the Golden Dawn, a few fundamental notions of the philosophy underlying its practise must be grasped. The basic theory of the Order system was such as to identify certain of the grades with various spiritual principles existing in the universe. Hence a philosophy which describes, classifies, and purports to understand the nature of the universe must be studied before the significance of the grades can be appreciated. One of the most important backgrounds of the system is the scheme of the

Qabalah, a Jewish system described at length in my *Tree of Life* and the knowledge lectures herein. Since it is primarily a mystical method, the Qabalah has innumerable points of identity with the more ancient systems elaborated by other peoples in other parts of the world. Its most important root concept is that the ultimate root from which this universe, with all things therein, has evolved in *Ain Soph Aour*, Infinite or Limitless Light. So far as our minds are capable of conceiving such metaphysical abstractions, this is to be understand as an infinite ocean of brilliance wherein all things were evolved, and it is that divine goal to which all life and all beings eventually must return.

Issuing from within this Boundless Light, there manifests what is called the Tree of Life. Qabalists have produced a conventional glyph indicating thereupon ten numerations or *Sephiroth* which are the branches of that Tree growing or evolving within space, ten different modes of the manifestation of its radiation–ten varying degrees of but one ubiquitous substance-principle.

The first of these numerations is called *Kether*, the Crown, and is the first manifestation from the Unknown, a concentration of its Infinite Light. As the radiant apex of this heavenly tree, it is the deepest sense of selfhood and the ultimate root of substance. It constitutes the divine centre of human consciousness, all the other principles which comprise what we call man being rather like so many layers of an onion around a central core. From this metaphysical and universal centre duality issues, two distinct principles of activity, the one named *Chokmah* Wisdom, and the other *Binah*, Understanding. Here we have the roots of polarity, male and female, positive and negative, fire and water, mind and matter, and these two ideas are the noumena of all the various opposites in life of which we have cognisance.

These three emanations are unique in a special way, and they especially symbolise that "Light which shineth in darkness," the Light of the spiritual Self. As Light shines into darkness, illuminating it without suffering shines into darkness, illuminating it without suffering a diminution of its own existence, so the workings of the Supernals, as these three Sephiroth are called, overflow from their exuberant being without thereby diminishing in any degree the reality or infinite vitality of their source. They are considered hence to have but little relation with the inferior Sephiroth which issue from them, except as stem and root. Yet though hardly in any philosophic relation to our phenomenal universe, we find when engaged in magical working that it is customary—even necessary—to open ourselves by invocation to its influence so that this divine power of the Supernal Light, descending through the human mind, may sanctify and accomplish the object of the ceremony itself. The Supernals are often portrayed diagrammatically and symbolically as a woman clothed with the Sun, stars above her head and the moon at her feet—the typical *anima* figure of modern psychology.

She represents thus that First Matter of the Alchemists, the description of which given by Thomas Vaughan in his *Coelum Terrae* is interesting to quote as indicating further the nature and qualities of the Supernals: "A most pure sweet virgin, for nothing as yet hath been generated out of her…She yields to nothing but love, for her end is generation, and that was never yet performed by violence. He that knows how to wanton and toy with her, the same shall receive all her treasures. First, she sheds at her nipples a thick heavy water, but white as any snow; the philosophers call it Virgin's Milk. Secondly, she gives him blood from her very heart; it is a quick, heavenly fire; some improperly call it sulphur. Thirdly and lastly, she presents him with a secret crystal, of more worth and lustre than the white rock and all her rosials. This is she, and these are her favours."

From this first triad, a second triad of emanations is reflected or projected downwards into a more coarse degree of substance. They likewise reflect the negative and positive qualities of two of the Supernals with the addition of a third factor, a resultant which acts as a reconciling principle. In passing, I should add that planetary attributions are given to these Sephiroth as expressing the type of their operation. *Kether* is Spirit, *Chokmah* refers to the Zodiac, the *Binah* is attributed to Saturn.

The fourth Sephirath is *Chesed*, meaning Grace or Mercy; also *Gedulah* is its other name, meaning Greatness, and to it is referred the astrological quality called Jupiter. Its concept is one construction, expansion and solidification.

Geburah is the fifth enumeration, Power or Might, and it is a symbol of creative power and force. Its planetary attribution is Mars, its quality being that destructive force which demolishes all forms and ideas when their term of usefulness and healthy life is done. It symbolises not so much a fixed state of things, as an act, a further passage and transition of potentiality into actuality.

Six is the harmonising and reconciling Sephirah, *Tiphareth*. The word itself means beauty and harmony. It is attributed to the Sun, the lord and centre of our solar system. Just as *Kether* referred to the most secret depths of the Unconscious, the core of man's life, so *Tiphareth* is its reflection, the ego, the ordinary human consciousness. This Sephirah completes the second triad, which is a triad of consciousness, as the first triad of the Supernal Light may be considered the triad of that which is supremely divine, the Superconscious.

Netsach, Victory, to which the planet Venus is referred, is the first Sephirah of the third reflected triad, and marks an entirely different order of things. Here we enter the elemental sphere, where Nature's forces have their sway. It is also the region in the human sphere of what we may term the Unconscious. The magical tradition classifies this Unconsciousness into several strata, and to each of them is attributed some one of the four elements, Fire, Water, Air and Earth. *Netsach* is attributed to the element of Fire, and so far as concerns the classification of man's principles, it represents his emotional life.

Its opposite pole on the Tree of Life, is *Hod*, which means Splendour, which receives the attribution of the planet Mercury. Its element is Water, and its action represents fluidic mind, the thinking, logical capacity in man, as well as what may be called his magical or nervous force–what the Hindu systems denominate as Prana.

The third of that triad is *Yesod*, the Foundation, the ninth Sephirah, the operation of the Sphere of the Moon. This is the airy sphere of the fourth dimension, termed in occultism the Astral plane. Here we find the subtle electro-magnetic substance into which all the higher forces are focussed, the ether, and it constitutes the basis or final model upon which the physical world is built. Its elemental attribution is that of Air, ever flowing, shifting, and in a constant flux–yet because of that flux, in perpetual stability. Just as the tremendous speed of the particles insure the stability of the atom, so the fleeting forms and motion of *Yesod* in all its implications constitute the permanence and surety of the physical world.

Pendant to these three triads in *Malkuth*, the Kingdom, referred to the element of Earth, the synthesis or vehicle of the other elements and planets. *Malkuth* is the physical world, and in man represents his physical body and brain, the Temple of the Holy Ghost–the actual tomb of the allegorical Christian Rosenkreutz.

These Sephiroth are not be construed as ten different portions of objective space, each separated by millions and millions of miles–though of course they must have their correspondences in different parts of space. They are, rather, serial concepts, each condition or state or serial concept enclosing the other. Each

Sephirah, be it spiritual, ethereal, or physical, has its own laws, conditions, and "times," if one may borrow terminology from Dunne's *Experiment with Time*. The distinction between them is one of quality and density of substance. The difference may well be one of dimension, besides representing different type-levels of consciousness, the "lower" worlds or Sephiroth being interpenetrated or held by the "higher." Thus *Kether*, the Crown, is in *Malkuth*, as one axiom puts it, by virtue of the fact that its substance is of an infinitely rare, attenuated, and ethereal nature, while *Malkuth*, the physical universe is enclosed within the all-pervading spirit which is *Kether* in precisely the same way that Dunne conceives Time No. 1, to be enclosed or contained, or moving as a field of experience, within Serial Time No. 2.

So far as concerns the Supernals, for these are the ideas which must principally interest us, the Qabalah teaches us that they comprise an abstract impersonal principle. That is, it is explained as an exalted condition of consciousness rather than of substance; an essence or spirit which is everywhere and at all times expressed in terms of Light. In one sense, and from a comparative point of view, it may help our understanding if we imagine it to have certain similarities to what our leading Analytical Psychologists call the Collective Unconscious.

Though wholly impersonal in itself, and without characteristics that are readily understandable to the ordinary mind, the Supernals are, to all intents and purposes, what is commonly thought of as God. In the Tibetan Buddhist system, an analogous concept is *Sunyata*, the Void. And the realisation of the Void through Yoga processes and the technical meditations of the Sangha is, to quote Dr. Evan-Wentz's book *The Tibetan Book of the Dead*, to attain "the unconditioned Dharmakaya, or the Divine Body of Truth, the primordial state of uncreatedness, of the Supramundane *Bodhic*, All-consciousness–Buddhahood." In man, this Light is represented by the very deepest levels of his Unconscious–a mighty activity within his soul, which one magical system calls the higher and Divine Genius. Though the Golden Dawn rituals persistently use phraseology which implies the belief in a personal God, that usage to my mind is a poetic or dramatic convention. A number of its very fine invocations are addressed to a deity conceived of in a highly individualistic and personal manner, yet if the student bears in mind the several Qabalistic definitions, these rituals take on added and profound meaning from a purely psychological point of view. That is, they are seen to be technical methods of exalting the individual consciousness until it comes to a complete realisation of its own divine root, and that universal pure essence of mind which ultimately it is.

It may be convenient for the reader if I tabulate the names of the Sephiroth with the Grades employed in the Golden Dawn, together with a few important attributions:

1.	*Kether.*	The Crown. Spirit.	Ipsissimus	⑩=[1]
2.	*Chokmah.*	Wisdom.	Magus	⑨=[2]
3.	*Binah.*	Understanding	Magister Templi	⑧=[3]
4.	*Chesed.*	Mercy.	Adeptus Exemptus	⑦=[4]
5.	*Geburah.*	Might.	Adeptus Major	⑥=[5]
6.	*Tiphareth.*	Harmony.	Adeptus Minor	⑤=[6]
7.	*Netzach.*	Victory. Fire.	Philosophus	④=[7]
8.	*Hod.*	Splendour. Water.	Practicus	③=[8]
9.	*Yesod.*	Foundation. Air.	Theoricus	②=[9]
10.	*Malkuth.*	Kingdom. Earth.	Zelator	①=[10]

In the consideration of the grades, I shall not discuss any others than those existing between Zelator and Adeptus Minor.

My reason for doing so is that it is impossible for the ordinary individual to understand those above the grade of Adeptus Minor, and individuals who lay claim openly to such exalted grades, by that very act place a gigantic question mark against the validity of their attainment. He that is exalted is humble. And to have tasted that which is conveyed by the Adeptus Minor grade is so lofty an experience that few in their right minds, unless they were extremely saintlike in character, would consider themselves as having passed officially to a higher spiritual state.

Before proceeding to an analysis of the grades, and the ceremonies which were supposed to confer them, it has been thought advisable to consider the nature of initiation itself, which was the avowed function and purpose of the Order. What exactly is Initiation? Those of us who have read of the neo-occult and pseudo-Theosophical literature will also have heard the word initiation just too often to feel wholly at ease. Lesser Initiations and Greater Initiations have been written of at some length. But the entire subject was surrounded with that vague air of mystery, that halo of sanctity and ambiguity whose only excuse can be ignorance on the part of the writers thereof. The degree of phantasy and attenuated sentimentality which has obtained expression from these sources, plus the real lack of knowledge as to the objects of these degrees and mysteries, act as a constant source of irritation. Particularly, when we remember that they were issued to satisfy people spiritually hungry, and yearning with an indescribable hunger for but a few crumbs of the divine wisdom.

Learned dissertations have been published describing in great detail the folk customs of Australian aborigines and Polynesian and other primitive peoples. All the strange habits and unfamiliar rites of these tribes are paraded before our gaze–from their hour of birth, through the vicissitudes of their emotional life, to the moment of death and interment. We are asked to accept that these are initiations. The sole import attached to the word "initiation" in this connection is that of the formal acceptance of a boy at puberty, for example, into the communal life of his people.

Moreover, Jane E. Harrison, Sir F. G. Frazer and a host of other excellent scholars have provided us with a wealth of anthropological data so far as the Greeks and Romans of another day are concerned. Some knowledge of their religious rites and observations is displayed. The daily habits of the people are carefully noted and recorded in many a tome.

They also describe, though more haltingly and with rather less confidence, the circumstances surrounding the Ancient Mystery Cults. The symbolism of these mystery religions was, we see, in certain aspects uniform. All were dramas of redemption, plans of salvation, ways of purgation. Degrees of initiation, baptism by water, a mystical meal for the privileged, dramatic plays depicting the life and death of some god or other–these are the familiar incidents of the cults described by our scholars.

But the obvious question arises, what spiritual value have such things for us? Do they help our own interior development so that we may solve our personal problems and handle more satisfactorily the rather difficult process of living to-day? And is this sort of thing what the Adepts of old implied by initiation? And if this is all there is to it, why should so many moderns have been so curiously perturbed and excited by it all. Some other meaning must be latent herein; some other purposed to the rite must have been understood by their original observers whereby they were spiritually assisted and aided not only to deal adequately with life but to further the conquest and manifestation of their own latent spiritual nature.

For despite every record, and every learned attempt to penetrate into the significance of these rites, as to the exact procedure of the Theurgic technique we still obtain no lasting satisfaction, or understanding. There was undoubtedly a secret about these celebrations, both ethnic and early Christian, which no exoteric record has divulged or common sense, so-called, succeeded wholly to explain away. And the reason no doubt it this. Though the early writers felt no hesitancy in expounding certain principles of the philosophy of their Mysteries, none felt it incumbent upon himself to record in black and white the practical details of the magical technique. Hence it is, in the absence of a description of the practical elements of these rites, that our scholars, anthropologists and philosophers do not feel inclined to attach much significance to the ancient Mysteries other than an ordinary religious or philosophic one. That is, it is their belief that ordinary notions of an advanced theological or philosophical nature were promulated therein. For I may add in passing the complete esoteric technique of initiation has never previously passed into open publication. It has been reserved in all secrecy for initiates of the sacred schools of Magic. While various documents explaining the principia of this wisdom were circulated amongst the members of these schools, the oaths of secrecy attaching to their receipt was such that in recent times, as I have said, few lay exponents of the ancient religions and philosophies have ever so much as suspected the existence of these principia.

The root of the word itself means "to begin," "to commence anew." Initiation is thus the beginning of a new phase or attitude to life, the entry, moreover, into an entirely new type of existence. Its characteristic is the opening of the mind to an awareness of other levels of consciousness, both within and without. Initiation means above all spiritual growth–a definite mark in the span of human life.

Now one of the best methods for bringing about this stimulus of the inner life, so that one does really begin or enter upon an entirely new existence characterised by an awareness of higher principles within, is the Ceremonial technique. By this we mean that a Ceremony is arranged in which certain ideas, teaching and admonitions are communicated to the candidate in dramatic form in a formally prepared Temple or Lodge room. Nor is this all–otherwise, no claim could be made on behalf of Magic that it really and not merely figuratively initiates. For the utterance of an injunction does not necessarily imply that it can sink sufficiently deeply into consciousness so as to arouse into renewed activity the dormant spiritual qualities. And we have already witnessed the invalidity and spiritual bankruptcy of innumerable organisations, religious, secular, and fraternal so-called, which have their own rituals and yet, taking them by and large, have produced very few initiates or spiritually-minded men and women, saints or adepts of any outstanding merit.

The efficacy of an initiation ceremony depends almost exclusively on the initiator. What is it that bestows the power of successful initiation? This power comes from either having had it awakened interiorly at the hands of some other competent initiator, or that a very great deal of magical and meditation work has successfully been performed. It is hardly necessary at this juncture to labour at a description of these exercises and technical processes of development which were undertaken by candidates and would-be initiators. These have been delineated at length elsewhere, both in my *Tree of Life*, and in an incomparably fine form in the Golden Dawn documents presented herein. But it is necessary to emphasise the fact that an anterior personal training and prolonged magical effort are the sole means by which on is enabled so to awaken the dormant spiritual life of another that he may well and truly be called "initiated."

Now we know from an examination of the above mentioned documents and of ancient literature that the object of the Theurgic art, as the magical concept of initiation was then termed, was to purify the personality that that which was there imprisoned could spring into open manifestation. As one of the alchemical expositors has expressed it: "Within the material extreme of this life, *when it is purified*, the Seed of the Spirit is at last found." The entire object of all magical and alchemical processes is the purification of the natural man, and by working upon his nature to extract the pure gold of spiritual attainment. This is initiation.

§

These Golden Dawn rituals and ceremonies of initiation are worthy of a great deal of study and attention. It is my sincere and fervent hope that meditation and a close examination will be made of the text. Now, if we examine these texts carefully, we shall find that we can epitomise in a single word the entire teaching and ideal of those rituals. If one idea more than any other is persistently stressed from the beginning that idea is in the word *Light*. From the candidate's first reception in the Hall of the Neophytes when the Hierophant adjures him with these words: "Child of Earth, long hast thou dwelt in darkness. Quit the night and seek the day," to the transfiguration in the Vault ceremony, the whole system has as it objective the bringing down of the Light. For it is by that Light that the golden banner of the inner life may be exalted; it is in light where lies healing and the power of growth. Some vague intimation of the power and splendour of that glory is first given to the aspirant in the Neophyte Grade when, rising from his knees at the close of the invocation, the Light is formulated above his head in the symbol of the White Triangle by union of the implements of the three chief officers. By means of the Adeptus Minor ritual, which identifies him with the Chief Officer, he is slain as though by destructive force of his lower self. After being symbolically buried, triumphantly he rises from the tomb of Osiris in a glorious resurrection through the descent of the white Light of the Spirit.

The intervening grades occupy themselves with the analysis of that Light as it vibrates between the light and darkness, and with the establishment within the candidate's personal sphere of the rays of the many-coloured rainbow of promise.

"Before all things," commences a phrase in one ritual, "are the chaos, the darkness, and the Gates of the Land of Night." It is in this dark chaotic night so blindly called life, a night in which we struggle, labour and war incessantly for no reasonable end, that we ordinary human beings stumble and proceed about our various tasks. These gates of the far-flung empire of the night indeed refer eloquently to the material bondage which we ourselves have created–a bondage whereby we are tied to our circumstances, to our selves, to trial of every kind, bound to the very things we so despise and hate. It is not until we have clearly realised that we are enmeshed in darkness, an interior darkness, that we can commence to seek for that alchemical solvent which shall disperse the night, and call a halt to the continual projection outwards of the blackness which blinds our souls. As in the Buddhist scheme, where the first noble truth is sorrow, so not until we have been brought by experience to understand life as sorrow, can we hope for cessation of its dread ravage. Only then does the prospect open of breaking the unconscious project, the ending of which discloses the world and the whole of life in a totally different light. "One thing only, brother, do I proclaim," said the Buddha, "now as before. Suffering and deliverance from suffering."

These restricting circumstances and bonds are only the gates of the wilderness. The use of the word "gate" implies a means both of egress and ingress. By these gates we have entered, and by them also may we go out if so we choose, to enter the brilliance of the dawning Sun, and perchance greet the rising of the spiritual splendour. For "after the formless, the void, and the darkness, then cometh the knowledge of the Light." As intimated above, one first must have realised that one's soul is lost in darkness before a remedy can be sought to that irresponsible *participation mystique*, the unconscious projection outwards of interior confusion, and aspire to that divine land which is, metaphorically, the place of one's birth. In that land is no darkness, no formlessness, no chaos. It is the place of the Light itself–that Light "which no wind can extinguish, which burns without wick or fuel."

Being "brought to the Light" then is a very apposite description of the function of Initiation. It is the Great Work. There is no ambiguity in the conception of the Rituals, for it appears throughout the entire work from Neophyte to Adeptus Minor and perhaps beyond. For the Path is a journeying upwards on the ladder of existence to the crown of the Tree of Life, a journey where every effort made and every step taken brings one a little nearer to the true glory of the Clear Light. As we know, the experience of the rising of the Light in both vision and waking state is common to mystics of every age and of every people. It must be an experience of the greatest significance in the treading of the Path because its appearance seems always and everywhere an unconditional psychic thing. It is an experience which defies definition, as well in its elementary flashes as in its most advanced transports. No code of thought, philosophy or religion, no logical process can bind it or limit it or express it. But always it represents, spiritually, a marked attainment, a liberation from the turmoil of life and from psychic complications and, as Dr. C. G. Jung has expressed the matter, it "thereby frees the inner personality from emotional and imaginary entanglements, creating thus a unity of being which is universally felt as a release." It is the attainment of spiritual puberty, marking a significant stage in growth.

Symptomatic of this stage of interior growth is the utter transformation that comes over what previously appeared to be "the chaos, the darkness, and the Gates of the Land of Night."

While man is assumed into godhead, and the divine spirit is brought down into manhood, a new heaven and a new earth make their appearance, and familiar objects take on a divine radiance as though illumined by an internal spiritual light. And this is what, in part at any rate, was meant by the old alchemists, for the finding of the Philosopher's Stone converts all base metals into the purest gold. In his book *Centuries of Meditation*, Thomas Traherne gives an interesting description of the rapture of the inner personality, its reaction to the world, when it is freed by the mystical experience from all entanglements. He says: "The corn was orient and immortal wheat, which never should be reaped, nor was ever sown. I thought it had stood be reaped, nor was ever sown. I thought it had stood from everlasting to everlasting. The dust and the stones of the street were as precious as gold; the gates were at first through one of the gates, transported and ravished me, their sweetness and unusual beauty made my heart to leap, and almost mad with ecstasy, they were such strange and wonderful things. The men! O what venerable and reverend creatures did the aged seem! Immortal Cherubim! And the young men glittering and sparkling angels, and maids, strange seraphic pieces of life and beauty. Boys and girls tumbling in the street, and playing, were moving jewels…I knew not that they were born or should die. But all things abided eternally as they in their proper places. Eternity was manifest in the Light of the Day, and something infinite behind everything appeared…"

And to illustrate the magical attitude towards life and the world when initiation has produced its true result, there is another exalted panegyric by Traherne which I cannot desist from quoting. For let me add that Magic does not countenance a retreat from life, an escape from the turmoils of practical life. It seeks only to transmute what formerly was dross into gold. Initiation has as its object the commencement of a new life, to transform the base and low into the pure and unutterably splendid. "All appeared new and strange at first, inexpressibly rare and delightful and beautiful. I was a little stranger which at my entrance into the world was saluted and surrounded with innumerable joys. My knowledge was Divine; I knew by intuition those things which since my Apostacy I collected again by the highest reason. My very ignorance was advantageous. I seemed as one brought into the state of innocence. All things were spotless and pure and glorious; yea, and infinitely mine and joyful and precious. I knew not that there were any sins, or complaints or laws. I dreamed not of poverties, contentions, or vices. All tears and quarrels were hidden from my eyes. Everything was at rest, free and immortal. I knew nothing of sickness or death or extraction. In the absence of these I was entertained like an angel with the works of God in their splendour and glory; I saw all in the peace of Eden... All Time was Eternity, and a perpetual Sabbath..."

Such is the stone of the Philosophers, the Quintessence, the Summum Bonum, true wisdom and perfect happiness.

Psellus, the Neoplatonist, has written that the function of Initiatory Magic was "to initiate or perfect the human soul by the powers of materials here on earth; for the supreme faculty of the soul cannot by its own guidance aspire to the sublimest intuition and to the comprehension of Divinity." It is a commonplace aphorism in Occultism that "Nature unaided fails." That is to say that the natural life, if left to itself, and isolated from the impact of a higher type of life or consciousness, can only produce a commonplace thing of the natural life. It reminds us of the sentiment of the alchemists who expressed contempt of their first matter as it existed in its natural or impure state, in the condition where it normally is found. But this first matter, cleansed and purified by the psycho-chemical art of alchemy, that is to say by Initiation–is that which is transformed into the most precious thing in the whole world.

But until cleansed and purified it is of little or no value. Nature, however, aided where she had left off by wise and devout men, may surpass herself. And this is who Psellus claims that the soul of itself and by itself is not able to attain to divinity unless and until it is guided by Initiates and thus enfolded into another life. It is to effect this integration, to bring about this initiation, this exaltation of the consciousness above its natural state to the light divine, that the magical system of the Golden Dawn, or of any other legitimate initiating system, owes its existence. The function of every phase of its work, the avowed intention of its principal rituals, and the explicit statement of its teaching, is to assist the candidate by his own aspirations to find that unity of being which is the inner Self, the pure essence of mind, the Buddha-nature. Not only does the system imply this by its ritualistic movements and axiomata, but there are clear and unmistakable passages where these ideas are given unequivocal expression. Thus, we find it written that the entire object of initiation and mystical teaching is "by the intervention of the symbol, ceremonial and sacrament, so to lead the soul that it may be withdrawn from the attraction of matter and delivered from the absorption therein, whereby it walks in somnambulism, knowing not whence it cometh nor whither it goeth." And moreover, in the same Ritual, celebrated at the autumnal and vernal Equinoxes, the Chief Adept officiating recites an invocation beseeching guidance for the newly-installed Hierophant. It is asked "that he may well and worthily direct those who have been called from the tribulation of the darkness into the Light of this little kingdom of Thy love. And vouchsafe also, that going forward in love for Thee, through him and with him, they may pass from the Desire of Thy house into the Light of Thy presence." This is succeeded by sentences read by the Second and Third Adepti: "The desire of Thy house hath eaten me up," and "I desire to be dissolved and to be with Thee."

And finally, that not the least vestige of misunderstanding or misconception may remain as to the objects of this divine Theurgy, let me reproduce one last quotation from this same ritual. Referring to the Supernals and the Temple that in old time was build on high, the speech adds: "The holy place was made waste and the Sons of the house of Wisdom were taken away into the captivity of the senses. We have worshipped since then in a house made with hands, receiving a sacramental ministration by a derived Light in place of the cohabiting Glory. And yet, amidst Signs and symbols the tokens of the Higher presence have never been wanting in our hearts. By the waters of Babylon we have sat down and wept, but we have ever remembered Zion; and that memorial is a witness testifying that we shall yet return with exultation into the house of our Father."

Thus and unmistakably is the true object of the Great Work set before us, and we shall do well ever to keep eye and aspiration firmly fixed thereto. For while the road to the spiritual Zion demands great exertion, and because it is a way that at times proceeds by devious routes, there is great temptation to linger by the roadside, to stroll down pleasant side-lanes, or to play absentmindedly with toys or staves cut but to assist our forward march. But if we forget not to what noble city the winding path leads us, little danger can overtake any who pursue it steadfast to the end. It is only when the abiding city is forgotten that the road becomes hard, and the way beset by unseen danger and difficulty.

Prior to attempting to describe a few of the salient points of the Rituals–briefly, for since they appear within these volumes, they must be individually studied and experienced so that an individual point of view may be acquired–it may be advisable to devote a few explanatory words to the Art of Ceremonial Initiation itself.

A useful and significant preface may be taken from Dr. Jung's commentary to Wilhelm's translation of *The Secret of the Golden Flower*, where there is much that explains the ritualistic functions of Magic. "Magical practices are," he declares, "the projections of psychic events which, in cases like these, exert a counter influence on the soul, and act like a kind of enchantment of one's own personality. That is to say, by means of these concrete performances, the attention or better said the interest, is brought back to an inner sacred domain which is the source and goal of the soul. This inner domain contains the unity of life and consciousness which, though once possessed, has been lost and must now be found again."

From one point of view the officers employed in these Rituals represent just such psychic projections. They represent, even as figures in dreams do, different aspects of man himself–personifications of abstract psychological principles inhering within the human spirit. Through the admittedly artificial or conventional means of a dramatic projection of these personified principle in a well-ordered ceremony a reaction is induced in consciousness. This reaction is calculated to arouse from their dormant condition those hitherto latent faculties represented objectivity in the Temple of Initiation by the officers. Without the least conscious effort on the part of the aspirant, an involuntary current of sympathy is produced by this external delineation of spiritual parts which may be sufficient to accomplish the purpose of the initiation ceremony. The aesthetic appeal to the imagination–quite apart from what could be called the intrinsic magical virtue from what could be called the intrinsic magical virtue with which the G.D. documents Z-1 and Z-3 deal at some length–stirs to renewed activity the life of the inner domain. And the entire action of this type of dramatic ritual is that the soul may discover itself exalted to the heights, and during that mystical elevation receive the rushing forth of the Light.

Applying these ideas then, to the Neophyte or _____–so called because it is not attributed to any of the enumerations or Sephiroth on the Tree of Life since it is a preliminary or probationary grade– we find that the Kerux is an officer who personifies the reasoning faculties. He represents that intelligent active part of the mind which functions ever in obedience to the Will–the Qabalistic *Ruach*, in a word. The higher part of that mind, the aspiring, sensitive, and the intuitive consciousness is represented by the Hegemon, who seeks the rising of the Light. And the Hierophant, in this initial ceremony of Neophyte, acts on behalf of the higher spiritual soul of man himself, that divine self of which too rarely, if ever at all, we come aware. "The essence of mind is intrinsically pure," is a definition of the Bodhisattva Sila Sutra, and it is this essential state of enlightenment, this interior Self, Osiris glorified through trial and perfected by suffering, which is represented by the Hierophant on the dais. He is seated in the place of the rising Sun, on the throne of the East, and with but two or three exceptions never moves from that station in the Temple. As the Qabalah teaches, the everlasting abode of the higher Self is in the Eden of Paradise, the supernal sanctuary which is ever guarded from chaos by the flaming sword of the Kerubim whirling every way on the borders of the abyss. From that aloof spiritual stronghold it gazes down upon its vehicle, the lower man, evolved for the purpose of providing it with experience–involved in neither its struggles or tribulations, yet, from another point of view, suffering acutely thereby. And seldom does that Genius leave its palace of the stars except when, voluntarily, the lower self opens itself to the higher by an act of sincerest aspiration or self-sacrifice, which alone makes possible the descent of the Light within our hearts and minds. Thus when the Hierophant leaves the Throne of the East, he represents that Higher Self in action, and as Osiris marks the active descent of the Supernal splendour. For he says, as he leaves the dais with want uplifted: "I come in the Power of the Light. I come in the Light of Wisdom. I come in the Mercy of the Light. The Light hath healing in its wings." And having brought the Light to the aspirant, he returns to his throne, as though that divine Genius of whom he is the symbol awaited the deliberate willing return of the aspirant himself to the everlasting abode of the Light.

Even in the communication of the usual claptrap of secret societies, the signs and grips, all these are explained solely in terms of the quest for the Light. Also the various groupings of officers and their movements in the Temple are not without profound meaning. These should be sought out, since they constantly reiterate the implicit purpose of the rite. Thus, at the altar, the three principal officers form about the candidate a Triad, representing in symbolic formation again the Supernal clear Light of the Void, and this also is represented by the number of the circumambulations about the confines of the Temple. The white cord bound thrice about the waist has reference to the same set of ideas. Even upon the altar of the Temple are symbols indicating the rise of Light. A red calvary cross of six squares as symbolic of harmony and equilibrium is placed above a white triangle–the emblem of the Golden Dawn. They form the symbol of the Supernal Sephiroth which are the dynamic life and root of all things, while in man they constitute that triad of spiritual faculties which is intrinsically pure essence of mind. Hence the triangle is a fitting emblem of the Light. And the place of the Cross above the Triangle suggests not the domination of the sacred spirit, but its equilibriation and harmony in the heart of man. Despite the fact that the whole of this intricate symbolism can hardly be realise by the candidate at the time of his initiation, its intrinsic value is such that unconsciously as an organised body of suggestion it is perceived and noted and strikes the focal centre.

We are taught by tradition that the entire object of the sacred rites was the purification of the soul so that its power could gradually dissolve the impediments of, and percolate through, the heavy body and opaque brain. "Know" says Synesius, "that the Quintessence and hidden thing of our stone is nothing else than our viscous celestial and glorious soul *drawn out of its minera by our magistery*." Hence the entire trend of the preliminary Neophyte grade of the Golden Dawn is towards the purification of the personality. It fulfills the testimony of the Hermetic Art so that the Light within could be fermented and perfected by the ceremonial method of initiation. Purification and consecration–this is the insistent and uncompromising theme caught by the candidate's ear. "Unpurified and unconsecrated thou canst not enter our sacred Hall!" Fire and water assist in these several consecrations until, eventually, the candidate is placed in the position of balanced power, between the two Pillars, where the first like is effected with his higher and divine Genius.

§

The Neophyte Ritual really stands by itself. It is an introductory ceremony shadowing forth all the major formulae and techniques. With the Adeptus Minor ritual it is concerned almost entirely with the Light itself. The five grades that are placed between them have as their object the awakening of the elemental bases of what develop into the instrument of the higher. Awakened and purified, they may be consecrated to the Great Work, in order that they may become worthy vehicles for the indwelling of the Light. First, however, it is necessary that they be awakened. For, psychological truism that it is, until their presence is realised their transmutation cannot be accomplished. In symbolic form and pageantry, the ceremony of each grade calls forth the spirits of a particular element. And as a steel placed in close proximity to a magnet receives some degree of its magnetism, and comparable to the electrical phenomenon of induction, so the presence of power induces power. Contact with the appropriate type of elemental force produces an identical type of reaction within the sphere of the Neophyte, and it is thus that growth and advancement proceeds. The speeches of the officers deal almost exclusively with the knowledge pertaining to that element and grade, and excerpts from fragmentary remains of the ancient Mysteries and from certain of the books of the Qabalah do much towards producing an impressive atmosphere.

The element offered for the work of transmutation in the Grade of Zelator is the earthly part of the Candidate. The ritual symbolically admits him to the first rung of that mighty ladder whose heights are obscured in the Light above. This first rung is the lowest sphere of the conventional Tree of Life, *Malkuth*, the *Sanctum Regnum*. To it are ascribed the first grade of Zelator, and the element of Earth. Herein, after the Earth elementals are invoked, the Candidate is ceremonially brought to three stations, the first two being those of evil and the presence divine. At each of these stations the Guardians reject him at the point of the sword, urging him in his unprepared state to return. His third attempt to go forward places him in a balanced position, the path of equilibrium, the Middle Way, where he is received. And a way is cleared for him by the Hierophant, who again represents the celestial soul of things. During his journey along that path, the stability of earth is established within him, that eventually it may prove an enduring temple of the Holy Spirit.

Some have criticised these elemental grades a little harshly and severely; others have rejected them entirely. In a letter sent to me from a former Praemonstrator of one G. D. Temple, these rituals too were condemned in that they were said to be simply a parade, redundant and verbose, of the occult knowledge that one of the Chiefs possessed at that time. In one sense, of course, what those critics claim is perfectly true. The principal formulae and teaching are concealed in the preliminary Neophyte Grade and that of Adeptus Minor. It is the development of the ideas in these ceremonies which constitutes the Great Work–the disclosure of the essence of mind, the invocation of the higher Genius. These, however, are the high ends and the final goals of the mystic term. Notwithstanding his limitations these are ultimates to which every man must work. Meanwhile, in order to render that attainment possible in its fullest sense, several important matters require attention. The personality must be harmonised. Every element therein demands equilibriation in order that illumination ensuing from the magical work may not produce fanaticism and pathology instead of Adeptship and integrity. Balance is required for the accomplishment of the Great Work. "Equilibrium is the basis of the soul." Therefore, the four grades of Earth, Air, Water and Fire plant the seeds of the microcosmic pentagram, and above them is placed, in the Portal ceremony, the Crown of the Spirit, the quintessence, added so that the elemental vehemence may be tempered, to the end that all may work together in balanced disposition. These grades are therefore an important and integral part of the work, despite shortsighted hostile criticism. To compare them, however, with those which precede and follow, is symptomatic of an intellectual confusion of function. It is rather as if one said that milk is more virtuous than Friday– which, naturally, is absurd. Yet similar comparisons in magical matters are constantly being made without exciting ridicule. It is obvious that different categories may not be so compared. The purpose of the Neophyte ritual is quite distinct from that of Zelator, and it is mistaken policy to compare them. What rightly could be asked is whether the Zelator and the other elemental grades accomplish what they purport to do. That is another matter. The consensus of experienced opinion is on the whole that they do, and I am content for the time being to accept that authority.

The candidate by these grades is duly prepared, so it is argued, to enter the immeasurable region, to begin to analyse and comprehend the nature of the Light which has been vouchsafed him. The first three elemental grades could be taken just as quickly as the candidate, at the discretion of the Chiefs, desired.

There were no requirements other than to indicate by examination that the appropriate meditations had been performed and certain items of Qabalistic knowledge necessary to the magical routine committed to memory.

Before proceeding further in the analysis of the grades, there is one rather fine prose passage in the Zelator grade which must be given here–a passage of beauty, high eloquence, and lofty significance. "And Tetragrammaton placed Kerubim at the East of the Garden of Eden and a Flaming Sword which turned every way to keep the path of the Tree of Life, for He has created Nature that man being cast out of Eden may not fall into the Void. He has bound man with the stars as with a chain. He allures him with scattered fragments of the Divine Body in bird and beast and flower. And He laments over him in the Wind and in the Sea and in the Birds. And when the times are ended, He will call the Kerubim from the East of the Garden, and all shall be consumed and become infinite and holy."

It would be a happy task, were it advisable, to devote several pages of this introduction to praising the excellence of what are called the four elemental prayers. Each one of the elemental Initiation ceremonies closes with a long prayer or invocation which issues, as it were, from the heart of the elements themselves. These must be silently read, continuously meditated upon and frequently heard fully to be appreciated, when the reader will find his own personal reactions crystallising. Recited by the Hierophant at the end of the ceremony, these prayers voice the inherent aspiration of the elements towards the goal they are striving in their own way to reach, for here they are conceived as blind dumb forces both within and without the personal sphere of man. They are given assistance by the human beings who, having invoked them and used their power, strive to repay in some way the debt owed to these other struggling lives.

The grade after the Earth ceremony is that of Theoricus. It is referred to the Ninth Sephirah on the Tree of Life, *Yesod*, the Foundation, and to it are attributed the sphere of the operation of Luna and the element Air. Here the candidate is conducted to the stations of the four Kerubim, the Angelic choir of Yesod. The Kerubim are defined in that ritual as the presidents of the elemental forces, the vivified powers of the letters of Tetragammaton operating in the Elements. Over each of these rules some one of the four letters of the mirific word and the Kerubim. It is always through the power and authority and symbol of the Kerub that the elemental spirits and their rules are invoked. In this ritual, as in all the others, important practical formulae of ceremonial magic are concealed.

At this juncture, of the ceremony, with the Airy elements vibrating about him and through him, the Zelator is urged to be "prompt and active as the Sylphs, but avoid frivolity and caprice. Be energetic and strong as the Salamanders but avoid irritability and ferocity. Be flexible and attentive to images, like the Undines, but avoid idleness and changeability. Be laborious and patient like the Gnomes, but avoid grossness and avarice. So shalt thou gradually develop the powers of thy soul and fit thyself to command the spirits of the elements."

In each of the grades, several drawings and diagrams are exhibited, each one conveying useful knowledge and information required in the upward quest. The Tarot Keys are also dealt with, as indicating pictorially the stages of that journey, and depicting the story of the soul. It may not be possible because of the exigencies of space to reproduce in these volumes as pack of Tarot cards based upon exoteric descriptions–though I should very much liked to have done so. But by using the Waite and the available French and Italian packs, and by comparing them with the accounts given in the rituals, the imagination of the reader will render this omission unimportant.

The third grade is that of Practicus referred to the Sephirah *Hod*, the Splendour, the lowest of the Sephiroth on the left hand side of the Tree, the Pillar of Severity. Its attributes refer to the sphere of the operation of Mercury, but more especially to the element of Water which in this ceremony is invoked to power and presence. As I have previously remarked, and it bears constant reiteration, the Tree of Life and the Qabalistic scheme as a whole should be carefully studied so that the aptness of the attributions both to the Sephiroth and the Paths may be fully appreciated. Two Paths lead to the Sphere of Splendour, the Path of Fire from Malkuth, and the Path of the reflection of the sphere of the Sun from Yesod. Water is germinative and maternal, whilst Fire is paternal and fructifying. It is from their interior stimulation and union, the alchemical trituration, that the higher life is born, even as has been said, "Except ye be baptised with water and the Spirit ye cannot enter the Kingdom of heaven."

Therefore in this grade, the Candidate is led to the sphere of stagnant water which by the presence of solar and fiery elements is vitalised and rendered a perfect creative base. Most of the speeches in this ritual are depicted as issuing from the Samothracian Kabiri, the deluge Gods, though the main body of the ritual consists of the sonorous and resonant versicles of the *Chaldaean Oracles*, the translation, I believe, of Dr. Westcott, with a few modifications authorised by Mathers. Briefly, the entire symbolism of the Practicus grade modifications authorised by Mathers. Briefly, the entire symbolism of the Practicus grade is summarised by the position of the altar of the principal Golden Dawn emblems so arranged that "the cross above the Triangle of the Waters." That also indicated the immediate task of the Candidate. At this juncture, too, the diagrams displayed begin to take on especial significance, and though their theme apparently is biblical in nature, accompanied by explanations in a curious phraseology consonant therewith, they are nevertheless highly suggestive, as containing the elements of a profound psychology. After this grade follows an automatic wait of three months, referred to the regimen of the elements, a period as it were of silent incubation, during which time the rituals were given to the candidate that he may make copies for his own private use and study.

The fourth grade of Philosophus carries the candidate one step further. The Sephirah involved is *Netsach*, Victory, to which is referred the operation of the planet Venus and the element of Fire, while the paths that connect to the lower rungs of the ladder are principally of a watery nature. Thus the elements encountered are of an identical nature with those of the preceding grade, but their order and power is quite reversed. Previously the water was predominant. Now the Fire rages and whirls in lurid storm, with water only as the complementary element whereon it may manifest, and in order that due equilibrium may be maintained, as it is written:–"The *Ruach Elohim* moved upon the face of the Waters." These two are the primary terrestrial elements which, intelligently controlled and creatively employed may lead eventually to the restoration of the Golden Age. By their transmutation a new paradise may be re-created from the darkness and chaos into which formerly it had fallen. For the Light may not legitimately be called forth upon man, nor dwell within him, until chaos has been turned into equilibrium of complete realisation and enlightenment. Not until order has been restored to the lower elements of his earthly kingdom, neither peace nor inner security may be his rightful lot.

The symbols depicted while traversing the Path of Peh, which joins the spheres of Fire and Water, indicate the results as it were of the first stages of the Path, for the Tarot card shown demonstrates the destruction of a Tower by lightning. The three holes blasted in the walls symbolise the Supernal Triad, the establishment of the divine through and following the destruction of the outer self. Though Fire and Water, warmth and moisture, are essentially creative, their stimulation within the being of the Neophyte draws his attention, perhaps for the first time, to the chaotic condition of his natural existence, and the complete psychic muddle into which his ignorance and spiritual impotence have stranded him. Evocative of the highest within his soul, these elements equally call forth that which is base and low. The result of the first step is analytical, an unbalancing, the levelling down of all that man formerly held true and holy–the chaos, the darkness, and the Gates of the Land of Night. An unhappy state, but a very necessary one if progress is to be made and if the preliminary chaos is to be transcended. From these ruins may be erected the new temple of Light, for it is always from the rubbish heap that are selected the materials for the manifestation of god-head. These symbols have a dual reference. Not only do they refer to the epochs of creative evolution whose memory has long since faded even from the visible memory of nature, but also to the recapitulations of these periods within personal progress on the Path. "The Aspirant on the threshold of Initiation," observes Crowley very aptly, "finds himself assailed by the 'complexes' which have corrupted him, their externalisation excruciating him, and his agonised reluctance to their elimination plunging him into such ordeals that he seems (both to himself and to others) to have turned from a noble and upright man into an unutterable scoundrel." These are the experiences and events which occur to every aspirant when initiation forces the realisation upon him that "all is sorrow." In fact, it is my belief that the criterion or hall mark of successful initiation is the occurrence of these or similar experiences. The whole universe, under the stimulation of the magical elements and inward analysis, seems to tumble like a pack of cards crazily about one's feet. This is the *solve* half of the alchemical *solve et coagula* formula.

Analysis must preceed synthesis. Corruption is the primitive base from which the pure gold of the spirit is drawn. Moreover the alchemical treatises are eloquent in their description of the poisonous nature of this condition which, though extremely unpleasant, is a highly necessary one, and success in its production is at least one symptom of good working. It is held that the highest results may not be obtained until this particular type of change has occurred. So far as the nature of the environment and the creative power of the personal self permits, the task implied by the *coagula* formula is to assemble them and remould them nearer tot he heart's desire. And here again, the alchemist are adamant in their insistence upon the aphorism that "Nature unaided fails." For the alchemist, so the tradition asserts, commences his work where Nature has left off. And were this *solvé* phenomenon to occur spontaneously in the course of nature, the result and the outcome– the coagulation of previously dissolved elements–would not be very dissimilar to that which previously existed. But with the technique of initiation, the chaos is lifted up and fermented so to speak, that from it, with the aid of the invoked white Light of the divine Spirit, a higher species of being, illumined and enlightened, may develop.

In two Altar diagrams–one called the Garden of Eden, shown in the Practicus grade, and the other called The Fall shown in the Philosophus grade, all these ideas are expanded and synthesized. They should be carefully studied and receive long meditation, for in them are many clues to the spiritual and psychological problems which beset the traveller on the Path, and they resume the entire philosophy of Magic. Many hints, moreover, which may be found useful as assisting meditation are contained in *The 'Curse' from a Philosophical Point of View* in the second volume of Blavatsky's *Secret Doctrine* in connection with the Prometheus myth and the awakening of Manas, mind.

Since both of these diagrams may be found reproduced in the body of the text very little by way of prolonged explanation need here be said. The first depicts a personified representation of the three fundamental principles in Man. Each of these is apparently separate, functioning independently on its own plane without co-operation with, because apparently unaware of, either the higher or the lower. Principally, it represents man in now departed morning of the race, in the primal rounds of evolutionary effort when self-consciousness had not yet been won by self-induced and self-devised efforts, and when peace and harmony prevailed both within and without by right of heritage rather than through personal labour. The diagram appears in the Water grade of Practicus, since Water is a fitting representation of this placid peace. At the summit of the diagram stands the Apocalyptic woman clothed with the Sun of glory, crowned with the twelve stars, and the moon lying at her feet. Her symbolism pertains to the supernal essence of mind, representing thus the type and symbol of the glittering Augoeides, the *Neschamah*. Speaking of an analogous psychological conception in his commentary to *The Secret of the Golden Flower*, Dr. C. G. Jung remarks that this figure represents "a line or principle of life that strives after superhuman, shining heights." At the base of the tree stands Eve, the *Nephesch* or unconscious who, in opposition to this divine Genius, stands for the dark "earthbound, feminine principle with its emotionality and instinctiveness reaching far back into the depths of time, and into the roots of physiological continuity." Between the two stands Adam, supported by the fundamental strength of Eve, the *Ruach* or Ego not yet awakened to a realisation of its innate power and possibility. From the larger point of view he represents the race as a whole and "is the personified symbol of the collective Logos, the 'Host', and of the Lords of Wisdom or the Heavenly Man, who incarnated in humanity." Otherwise he represents the individual

Candidate on the Path, prior to the awakening of the "sleeping dogs" within his being, to use Blavatsky's apt expression.

Beneath these three figures sleeps a coiled dragon, silent, unawakened. None it would seem is aware of that latent power, titanic and promethean, coiled beneath—the active magical power centered in man, his libido, neutral, of vast potentialities but neither good nor evil in itself.

Very similar in some respects is the diagram revealed in the Philosophus Grade. As the divine peace of the garden of Eden was manifested during the Water grade, so in this Grade of Philosophus, the power of Fire is shown to have called forth catastrophe. Formerly called beneath the tree, the hydra-headed dragon in this Diagram has usurped its proper place. Its several horned heads wind their way up into the very structure of the Tree of Life, even under *Daath* at the foot of the Supernals. Lured downwards by the tree of knowledge—and remembering in what sense the Bible speaks of the verb "to know," we gather that the root of the trouble was an imperfect apprehension of creative power—towards the "darkly splendid world wherein continually lieth a faithless depth," Eve, the lower self, ceases to give support to Adam. She has yielded to the awful fascination of the awakening psyche. Far easier is it to fall than to climb to the distant heights. Yet only from one viewpoint is the Fall catastrophic. The awareness of the rise of the Dragon endows man also with consciousness of power—and power is life and progress. The Dragon stands as the symbol of the great enemy to be overcome, and, as the task of equilibration proceeds, the great prize awaiting success.

The Fall as a state of consciousness is analagous to that condition described by various mystics as the dark Night of the Soul. It is accompanied by a sense of intolerable dryness, a dreaded awareness of the fact that all the powers of the soul seem dead, and the mind's vision closed in dumb protest, as it were, against the harsh discipline of the Work itself. A thousand and one seductions will tend to lure the candidate from the contemplation of the magical goal, and there will be presented to him a thousand and one means of breaking in spirit his vow "to preserve in the divine science" without breaking it in letter. And it will appear that the mind itself will run riot and become unstable, warning the candidate that it were better for him to enjoy a lull in his magical operations. This state is allegorically referred to by the alchemists in their descriptions of the poisonous Dragon which follows upon the corruption of their First Matter. Vaughan calls it: "a horrible devouring Dragon–creeping and weltering in the bottom of her cave, without wings. Touch her not by any means, not so much as with thy hands, for there is not upon earth such a violent, transcendent poison." But as the mystics teach, if this condition be patiently endured, it passes, a higher spiritual consciousness gradually dawning in the heart and mind. So also in the alchemical writings, we find that Vaughan observes: "As thou hast begun so proceed, and this Dragon will turn to a Swan, but more white than the hovering virgin snow when it is not yet sullied with the earth."

The Qabalistic Sephirah of *Daath* is the conjunction of Chokmah and Binah on the Tree of Life, the child of Wisdom and Understanding–knowledge. It refers to the symbolic sphere formed within or above the Ruach by means of experience obtained, and this assimilated becomes transmuted into intuition and faculty of mind. But fundamentally it is the ascent of the Dragon or, if you wish, an upwelling of the Unconscious archetypes–a highly dangerous and unbalancing ascent, until they are assimilated to consciousness–which first renders *Daath* a possibility. It is the Fall which is responsible for the acquisition of self-knowledge. "Thus it stands proven" claims Blavatsky, "that Satan, or the red *Fiery* Dragon, the 'Lord of Phosphorus' and *Lucifer*, or 'Lightbearer,' is in us; it is our Mind–our temptor and Redeemer, our intelligent liberator and saviour from pure animalism."

In the evolutionary scheme, the Fall occurs through a higher type of intelligence coming into close contact with nascent humanity, thus stimulating the psyche of the race–or so the magical tradition has it. The recapitulation of this process within the individual sphere of consciousness of this process through the technique of initiation whereby the Red Dragon is stirred into activity through contact with the fructifying powers of a trained initiator. The use of the divine prerogative, brought about by the magic of every-day experience, the awakening of *Daath*, brings disaster at first because the awakened psyche is imperfectly understood and so abused for personal ends. But that very disaster and that abuse confers the consciousness of self, and is instrumental, at least in part of breaking up the primitive *participation mystique*. Consequently, the realisation of sorrow as it impinges on the ego, or at least the sense of personal mental and emotional discomfort, and an understanding of its causes, invariably constitute the first impetus the Great Work, even as it comprises the motive first to seek the services and aid of the analytical psychologist. This impetus and this self-consciousness are the prime implications of *Daath*. Its signification is a higher type of consciousness, the beginning of a spiritual rebirth. It acts as a self-evolved link between the higher Genius, on the one hand, at peace in its Supernal abode, and, on the other hand, the human soul bound by its Fall to the world of illusion and sense and matter. Not until that self-consciousness and acquired knowledge are turned to noble and altruistic ends, so long will sorrow and suffering be the inevitable result. Continually will the Red Dragon, the inverted power of the eros, ravish the little kingdom of self until such time as we open ourselves to the deepest levels of our unconsciousness, reconciling and uniting them with our conscious outlook, thus conquering the foe by driving it back to its proper realm. In such a way may we use, and its fruit to transcend our own personal limitations and attain to a *participation mystique* on a higher and self-conscious level.

Let me quote a few especially appropriate lines from Jung in connection with this Fall, when the fundamental basis of the *Ruach* has been attracted to the kingdom of shells and when *Malkuth* has been dissociated from the other Sephiroth: "Consciousness thus torn from its roots and no longer able to appeal to the authority of the primordial images, possesses a Promethean freedom, it is true, but it also partakes of the nature of a godless hybris. It soars above the earth, even above mankind, but the danger of capsizing is there, not for every individual to be sure, but collectively for the weak members of such a society, who again Promethean-like, are bound by the unconscious to the Caucasus."

For the Adept to be cut off from his roots, from contact with the vitalising and necessary basis of his Unconsciousness, will never do. He must unite and integrate the various levels of his entire Tree. His task must be a train and develop the titanic forces of his own underworld, so that they may become as a powerful but docile beast whereon he may ride.

§

The Adeptus minor grade continues the theme of these two diagrams. Escorted into the Vault, the Aspirant is shown the lid of the Tomb of Osiris, the Pastos, wherein is buried the Father, Christian Rosenkreutz, and on that lid is a painting which brings fulfilment as it were to the narrative of the preceding diagrams. It is divided into two sections. The lower half of the painting depicts a figure of Adam, similar to his presentation in the Practicus grade diagram, though here the heads of the Dragon are falling back from the Tree, showing the Justified One, the illuminated adept, by his immolation and self-sacrifice rescuing the fallen kingdom of his natural self from the clutches of an outraged eros. But above this, as though to show the true nature behind the deceptive appearance of things is illustrated a noble figure of majesty and divinity described in the Ritual in these words. "And being turned I saw seven golden Light-bearers, and in the midst of the Light-bearers, one like unto the Ben Adam, clothed with a garment down to the feet, and girt with a golden girdle. His head and his hair were white as snow, and his eyes as flaming fire; his feet like unto fine brass as if they burned in a furnace. And his voice as the sound of many waters. And he had in his right hand seven stars and out of his mouth went the Sword of Flame, and his countenance was as the Sun in his strength."

It is to effect this redemption of the personality, to regenerate the power of the dragon, and attempt to bring the individual to some realisation of his potential godhead, that his the object of the Adeptus Minor Ceremony.

It is for this reason that I hold that the Golden Dawn magic, the technique of initiation, is of supreme and inestimable importance to mankind at large. In it the work of academic psychology may find a logical conclusion and fruition, so that it may develop further its own particular contribution to modern life and culture. For this psycho-magical technique of ceremonial initiation indicates the psychological solution of the *anima* problem. "Arise! Shine! For thy light is come!"

Between the grade of Philosophus and the Portal, an interval of seven months was prescribed, the regimen of the planets. During that period, devised to assist the gradual fructification of the seeds planted within, a review was advised of all the preceding studies. Such a review certainly was imperative. As one of the Chiefs of the Order expressed it:–"Remember that there is hardly a circumstance in the rituals even of the First Order which has not its special meaning and application, and which does not conceal a potent magical formula. These ceremonies have brought thee into contact with certain forces which thou has now to learn to awaken in thyself, and to this end, read, study and re-read that which thou hast already received. Be not sure even after the lapse of much time that thou hast fully discovered all that is to be learned from these. And to be of use unto thee, this must be the work of thine own inner self, thine own and not the work of another for thee so that thou mayest gradually attain to the knowledge of the Divine Ones."

The Grade of the Portal, which conferred upon the Candidate of the title of Lord of the Paths of the Portal of the Vault of the Adepti, is not referred to a Sephirah as such. It may, however, be considered as an outer court to Tiphareth, exactly as the Adeptus Minor ceremony may be considered Tiphareth within. Its technical attribution is the element of Akasa, Spirit or Ether which is magically invoked by the usual procedure of invoking pentagrams and the vibration of divine names following upon the conjuration of the powers of the four subsidiary elements. To this grade, there is attached no elemental prayer as in the former grades, but there is one remarkable invocation employed which bears quoting here. In full Temple, the English version is not used, but it is vibrated in the original Enochian or Angelic tongue–a language which is at once sonorous, vibrant and dramatically impressive. The following is the full version of which an abridged one was normally used in the Temple: "I reign over you, (here the Order names the three Archangels of the elements) saith the God of Justice in power exalted above the firmament of wrath. In whose hands the Sun is as a sword and the Moon as a through thrusting fire. Who measureth your garments in the midst of my vestures and trussed you together as the palms of my hands. Whose seat I garnished with the fire of gathering. Who beautified your garments with admiration. To whom I made a law to govern the holy ones, and delivered you a rod with the ark of knowledge. Moreover, ye lifted up your voices and aware obedience and faith to him that liveth and triumpheth. Whose beginning is not nor end cannot be. Who shineth as a flame in the midst of your palaces and reigneth amongst you as the balance of righteousness and truth. Move therefore and show yourselves. Open the mysteries of your creation. Be friendly unto me, for I am the servant of the same your God, a true worshipper of the Highest."

This grade, referred to the veil *Paroketh*, which separates the First and Second Orders, is intermediate between the purely elemental grades and the spiritual grade of Adeptus Minor. A crown to the four lower element, this Rite formulates above Earth, Air, Water and Fire, the uppermost point of the Pentagram, revealing the administration of the Light over and through the kingdom of the natural world. It concerns itself with the recapitulation of the former grades, co-ordinating and equilibriating the elemental self which, symbolically sacrificed upon the mystical altar, is offered to the service of the higher Genius. In that grade, too, aspiration to the divine is strongly stressed as the faculty by which the veil of the inner sanctuary may be rent. It is the way to realisation. The five Paths leading from the grades of the First to the Second Orders are symbolically traversed, and their symbols impressed within the sphere of sensation.

A gestation period of at least nine months had to elapse prior to initiation to the grade of Adeptus Minor, and since there can be no misunderstanding the purpose and nature of this beautiful ceremony it requires the minimum of comment from my pen. It explains itself completely in one of the speeches: "Buried with that Light in a mystical death, rising again in a mystical resurrection, cleansed and purified through him our Master, o brother of the Cross of the Rose. Like him, o Adepts of all ages, have ye toiled. Like him have ye suffered through; they have been but the purification of the gold. In the alembic of thine heart through the athanor of afflication, seek thou the true stone of the wise."

The form of this ritual is beautiful in its simplicity and warrants a brief description. First of all, the candidate is led in, arrayed with insignia and badges and calling himself by his various titles and mottoes. But he is warned that not in any vainglorious spirit are the mysteries to be approached, but in simplicity alone. This is the signal for him to be divested of all his ornaments and insignia, and by the Temple entrance, just prior to being bound upon a large understanding cross of wood, he stands alone, clad in a simple unornamented black gown. The reader is earnestly recommended to study this Ritual again, and again, until almost it becomes a part of his very life, incorporated into the fabric of his being, for herein are highly important and significant formulae of mystical aspiration and of practical magic. In it is exemplified the technical "Dying God" formula about which in *The Golden Bough* Frazer has written so eloquently. Examples of this are to be found in every mythology and every mystical religion that our world has ever known. But I doubt that it has ever attained to a more clarified and definite expression than in this ceremony of the Adeptus Minor grade. For we are clearly taught by precept and by example that we are, in essence, gods of great power and spirituality who died to the land of our birth in the Garden of Hesperides, and mystically dying descend into hell. And moreover the ritual demonstrates that like Osiris, Christ, and Mithra, and many another type of god-man, we too may rise from the tomb and become aware of our true divine natures. The principal clause of the lengthy Obligation assumed while bound to the cross, indicating the trend of its teaching, and the import of its objective, is: "I further solemnly promise and swear that, with the Divine permission, I will from this day forward apply myself unto the Great Work, which is so to purify and exalt my spiritual nature that with Divine aid I may at length attain to be more than human and thus gradually raise and unite myself to my higher and divine Genius, and that in this event, I will not abuse the great power entrusted to me."

The preface to the assumption of the obligation is under these circumstances a tremendously impressive is under these circumstances a tremendously impressive occurrence, and few could fail to be even faintly moved by it. It consists of an invocation of an Angelic power: "In the divine name IAO, I invoke Thee thou great avenging Angel HUA, that thou mayest invisibly place thy hand upon the head of this Aspirant in attestation of his obligation..."

It is not difficult to realise that this is a critical and important phase of the ceremony. During this obligation, because of the symbolism attached to it and because of the active aspiration which is induced at this juncture, illumination may quite easily occur. In one of the documents describing certain effects ensuing from this initiation, one of the Chiefs has written, that the object of ceremony conceived as a whole "is especially intended to effect the change of the consciousness into the *Neschamah*, and there are three places where this can take place. The first is when the aspirant is on the cross, because he is so exactly fulfilling the symbol of the abnegation of the lower self and the Union with the higher."

The Obligation assumed, the candidate is now removed from the cross, and the Officers then narrate to him the principal facts in the history of the founder of the Order–Christian Rosenkreutz. On a previous page was given a summary of these historical facts. When the History lecture mentions the discovery of the Vault wherein the Tomb and body of the illustrious Father were discovered, one of the initiating adepts draws aside a curtain, admitting the candidate to a chamber erected in the midst of the Temple similar to that described in the lecture. A few words roughly describing it may not be considered amiss. As a climax to the very simple Temple furniture of the Outer grades, it comes as a psychological spasm and as a highly significant symbol.

The vault itself is a small seven-sided chamber, each side representing one of the seven planets, with their host of magical correspondences. The mediaeval Rosicrucian manifesto the Fama Fraternitatis, translated in Arthur Edward Waite's *Real History of the Rosicrucians*, describes it as great length, though I shall here quote but briefly: "We opened the door, and there appeared to our sight a vault of seven sides and seven corners, every side five foot broad and the height of eight foot. Although the sun never shineth in this vault, nevertheless it was enlightened with another Sun, which had learned this from the sun, and was situated in the upper part of the centre of the ceiling. In the midst, instead of a tombstone, was a round altar...Now, as we had not yet seen the dead body of our careful and wise Father, we therefore removed the altar aside; then we lifted up a strong plate of brass, and found a fair and worthy body, whole and unconsumed..."

Around this fundamental symbolism, the Golden Dawn adepts, displaying a genius of extraordinary insight and synthesis, had built a most awe-inspiring superstructure. The usual Order symbolisim of the Light was represented by a white triangle centered by the Rose–this placed upon the ceiling. The floor design was so painted as to represent the Red Dragon and the forces of the primitive archetypes upon which the candidate trod as emblematic of his conquest. Placed in the centre of the Vault was the Pastos of Rosenkreutz–though the Pastos is also referred to as the Tomb of Osiris the Justified One. Both of these beings may be considered as the type and symbol of the higher and divine Genius. Immediately above this coffin rested the circular altar mentioned in the Fama. It bore paintings of the Kerubic emblems, and upon these were placed the four elemental weapons and a cross, the symbol of resurrection. At one point in the ceremony, the acting Hierophant, or Chief Adept as he is now called, is interred in the Pastos as though to represent the aspirant's higher Self which is hidden and confined within the personality, itself wandering blindly, lost in the dark wilderness. The whole concatenation of the central theme of the Great Work. In a word, it depicts the spiritual rebirth or redemption of the candidate, his resurrection from the dark tomb of mortality through the power of the holy Spirit.

In the symbol of the Vault, the psychologist no doubt will see a highly interesting and complex array of Mother symbols, traces of which, used in very much the same way, may be found in the literary fragments were inherit from the mystery cults of antiquity. It would be possible, and quite legitimate so to interpret the Vault. For even the Order interpretation refers the Vault in its entirety to the Isis of Nature, the great and powerful mother of mankind and all that is. And an analysis of the separate parts of the Vault–the Venus door, the Pastos, the two Pillars–would subscribe to that view. For regeneration and the second birth have always as creative psychological states been associated with the Mother. And it may be recalled that the *Neschamah* or that principle in man which constantly strives for the superhuman shining heights, is always portrayed as a feminine principle, passive, intuitive and alluring. Whilst the universal counterpart of this human principle, represented on the Tree of Life by the Supernals, is always described by the mediaeval alchemists as a virginal figure, from whose life and substance all things have issued, and through whose agency man is brought to the second birth.

The reader is earnestly recommended to study this Ritual again and again until almost it becomes a part of his very life, incorporated into the very fabric of his being. Very little aesthetic appreciation will be required to realise that in this and the other rituals are passages of divine beauty and high eloquence. And the least learned will find ideas of especial appeal to him, as the scholar and the profound mystic will perceive great depth and erudition in what may appear on the surface as simple statement. Properly performed, with initiated technique and insight, these rituals are stately ceremonies of great inspiration and enlightenment.

The apparent complexity and the profound mystic will perceive great depth and erudition in what may appear on the surface as simple statement. Properly performed, with initiated technique and insight, these rituals are stately ceremonies of great inspiration and enlightenment.

The apparent complexity of the above delineated scheme may be thought by some individuals to be entirely too complicated for modern man and not sufficiently simple in nature. While one can deeply sympathise with the ideas of the extreme simplicity cult in Mysticism, nevertheless it is evident that the complex and arduous nature of the routine is no fault of Magic. Man himself is responsible for this awkward situation. To be purified was considered by the alchemists and the Theurgists of a bygone day as not nearly enough. That purification and consecration was required to be repeated and repeated, again and again. Because of countless centuries of evolution and material development–sometimes in quite false directions–man has spiritually repressed himself, and thus gradually forgotten his true divine nature. Meanwhile, as a sort of compensation for this loss, he has developed a complexity of physical and psychic constitution for dealing adequately with the physical world. Hence, methods of spiritual development refusing to admit the reality of that many-principled organisation may not be recognised as valid, for the sole reason that man is not a simple being. Fundamentally and at root he may be simple; but in actuality he is not. Having strayed from his roots, and lost his spiritual birthright in a jungle of delusion, it is not always easy to re-discover those roots or to find the way out from the Gates of the Land of Night.

In contradistinction to the above mentioned type of amorphous mystical doctrine, Magic *does* recognise the many-faceted nature of man. If that intricate structure so painfully constructed be considered an evil, as some seem to think, it is a necessary evil. It is one to be faced and used. Therefore Magic connives by its technique to use, develop, and improve each of these several principles to its highest degree of perfection. "Thou must prepare thyself" councils Vaughan "till thou art conformable to Him Whom thou wouldst entertain, and that in every respect. Fit thy roof to thy God in what thou canst, and in what thou canst not He will help thee. When thou hast thus set thy house in order, do not think thy Guest will come without invitation. Thou must tire Him out with pious importunities.

> Perpetual knockings at His door,
> Tears sullying his transparent rooms,
> Sigh upon sighs; weep more and more–
>   He comes.

This is the way thou must walk in, which if thou must walk in, which if thou dost thou shalt perceive a sudden illustration, and there shall then abide in thee fire with light, wind with fire, power with wind, knowledge with power, and with knowledge an integrity of sober mind!"

Not enough is it to be illuminated. The problem is not quite as simple as that. It is in vain that the wine of Gods is poured into broken bottles. Each part of the soul, each elemental aspect of the entire man must be strengthened and transmutted and brought into equilibrium and harmony with the others. Integration must be the rule of the initiate, not pathology. In such a vehicle made consecrate and truly holy by this equilibration, the higher Genius may find a worthy and fit dwelling. This and this alone, may ever constitute the true nature of initiation.

§

With each of the grades just described, a certain amount of personal work was provided, principally of a theoretical kind. The basic ideas of the Qabalah were imparted by means of so-called knowledge lectures, together with certain important symbols and significant names in Hebrew were required to be memorised. The lamens–insignia worn over the heart–of the various Officers were referred in divers ways to the Tree of Life, thus explaining after a fashion the function of that particular office in the Temple of Initiation. Each path traversed, and every grade entered, had a so-called Admission Badge. This usually consisted of one of the many forms of the Cross, and of symbols of the type of the Swastika, truncated Pyramid, and so forth. To these astrological and elemental attributions were referred. Most of these symbols possess great value, and since they repeated recur under different guises through the stages of personal magical work undertaken after the Adeptus Minor grade, they should receive the benefit of prolonged brooding and meditation.

Three of the most important items of personal study to be accomplished while in the First or Outer Order, apart from the memorisation of the rudiments of the Qabalah were: (a) The practice of the Pentagram Ritual with the Qabalistic Cross, (b) Tatwa Vision, and (c) Divination by Geomancy and the simple Tarot method described by Waite in his *Key to the Tarot*.

The Pentagram Ritual was taught to the Neophyte immediately after his initiation in order that he might "form some idea of how to attract and come into communication with spiritual and invisible things." Just as the Neophyte Ceremony of admission contains the essential symbolism of the Great Work, shadowing forth symbolically the commencement of certain formulae of the Magic of Light, so potential within the Pentagram Ritual and the Qabalistic Cross are the epitomes of the whole of that work. In all magical procedure it is fundamental, for it is a gesture of upraising the human consciousness to its own root of perfection and enlightenment by which the sphere of sensation and every act performed under its surveillance are sanctified. Thus it should precede every phase of magical work, elementary as well as advanced. The written rubic has previously appeared in my *Tree of Life*, and I may now add a word or two concerning the further directions which are orally imparted to the Candidate after his admission.

The prime factor towards success in that exercise is to imagine that the astral form is capable of expansion, that it grows tall and high, until at length it has the semblance of a vast angelic figure, whose head towers amongst the distant stars of heaven. When this imaginative expansion of consciousness produces the sense that the height is enormous, with the Earth as a tiny globe revolving beneath the feet, then above the head should be perceived or formulated a descending ray of brilliant Light. As the candidate marks the head and then the breast, so should this brilliance descend, even down to his feet, a descending shaft of a gigantic cross of Light. The act of marking the shoulder right and left whilst vibrating the Sephirotic names, traces the horizontal shaft of the cross, equilibriating the Light within the sphere of sensation. Since it has been argues above that the Great Work consists in the search for the Light, this ritual truly and completely performed leads to the accomplishment of that Work and the personal discovery of the Light. The Pentagrams trace a cleansing and protecting circle of force invoked by the four Names of four letters each about the limits of the personal sphere, and the Archangels are called, by vibration, to act as great stabilising influences.

The study of the different types of divination may seem difficult to understand in an Order which purported to teach methods of spiritual development. Many will no doubt be rather perplexed by this. Divination usually is said to refer exclusively to the low occult arts, to fortune-telling, and the prognostication of the future. Actually, however, so far as the Order is concerned, the principal object for these practical methods is that they stimulate, as few exercises can, the faculties of clairvoyance, imagination, and intuition. Though certain readings or interpretations to the geomantic and Tarot symbols may be found in the appropriate text books, these rule of thumb methods do not conduce to the production of an accurate delineation of the spiritual causes behind material events. These interpretations are usual to the beginner in the art, for he requires a foundation of the principal definitions employed upon which his own meditations can build. These textual delineations in actual practice serve only as a base for the working of the inner faculties, provides for them a thrust-block as it were from which they may "kick-off." In short, the effort to divine by these methods calls into operation the intuitive and imaginative faculties to a very large extent. Everyone without exception has in his ability to make it manifest. In most people it is wholly dormant.

Again, while divination as an artificial process may be wholly unnecessary and a hindrance to the refined perceptions of a fully developed Adept, who requires no such convention to ascertain whence a thing comes and whither it is going, yet these aids and stimuli have their proper place for the Neophyte. For those in training they are not only legitimate but useful and necessary. It may be interesting for the reader to attempt to acquire intuitive knowledge on any matter without the divinatory aids first, and it will be seen how extremely difficult it is to get started, to pick upon any one fact or incident which shall act as a prompt or a starter of the interior mechanism. Having failed in this way, let him see how much further he really may go by the judicious and sensible use of one of the Order methods. There is no doubt that the opening of the mind to an intuitive perception is considerably aided by these methods. And this is particularly true with regard to the rather lengthy Tarot method which was given to the initiate while engaged in the fulfillment of his Adpetus Minor curriculum. Like all magical techniques, divination is open to abuse. The fact, however, that abuse is possible does not, as again and again must be reiterated, fully condemn the abused technique. The application of common sense to the magical art is as necessary as it is to all else.

There was a movement on foot in one of the Temples a little while ago to eliminate the study and practice of Geomancy while ago to eliminate the study and practice of Geomancy from the scheme of training of the Outer Order. The prevailing tendency is so to simply the road to Adeptship as to reduce the practical requisites to an absolute minimum by eliminating every phase of the work which does not come "naturally," and whose study might involve hard work. Most of the newly admitted candidates to this Temple within the past five years more are utterly without any practical acquaintance with this technique.

Originally, Astrology was taught as part of the regular routine. All instruction on this subject seems now to have been thoroughly extirpated from the Order papers. Perhaps in this particular instance the omission is just as well. For recent years have seen a great deal of meticulous attention paid to this study by sincere and honest researchers, and there have been published many first-rate books explaining it intricacies. All that the Order demands of the Adeptus Minor is that he should be able to draw up a map showing the position of Planets and Signs, preparatory to certain operations requiring the invocation of zodiacal forces.

Tatwa vision requires but little mention in this place, for full instructions in this technical method of acquiring clairvoyance may be seen in a later volume. They are compiled from a number of documents and verbal instructions obtaining within the Order. Since these oral "tit-bits" and papers were very scattered, it has been found necessary to reorganise the whole matter. In that restatement, however, I have exercised no originality nor uttered personal viewpoints on any phase of the technique, confining my labour solely to re-writing, the material in my possession. It may be interesting for the psychological critic to reflect upon the fact that it was this technique to which most members of the Order devoted the greatest attention–the only technique in which, more than any other single branch of the work, there is greater opportunity for deception and self-deception. While in many ways the Order technique may appear different from the vision method described in my *Tree of Life*, both are essentially the same. For they teach the necessity of an imaginative formation of an intellectual or astral form, the Body of Light, for the purpose of exploring the different regions of the Tree of Life or the several strata of one's own psychic make-up. The simpler aspects of this investigation are taught just after the grade of Philosophus, though naturally the full possibilities of this method and the complete details on the technical side do not reveal themselves until the teaching of the Second Order has been received.

In addition to these technical methods there were meditations on the symbols and ideas of the whole system, and it was quite frequently suggested that the student go through the ceremonies, after having taken the grades, and build them up in his imagination so that he re-lives them as vividly as when he was in the Temple. The practical exercise that accompanied the Portal grade was one in which the aspirant built up, again in the imagination, a symbolic form of the Qabalistic Tree of Life, paying at first particular attention to the formulation of the Middle Pillar in the sphere of sensation or aura. This latter was conceived to be an ovoid shape of subtle matter, and the imaginative formulation of the various Sephiroth therein whilst vibrating the appropriate Divine Names went far towards opening, in a safe and balanced way, the psycho-spiritual centres of which the Sephiroth were but symbols. This technique, with the so-called Vibratory Formula of the Middle Pillar which is a development therefrom, I consider to be one of the most important practical systems employed in the Order. Though the documents describe it in a very rudimentary and sketchy fashion, nevertheless it is capable of expansion in several quite astonishing directions. I have discussed and expanded this technique at considerable length in my book *The Art of True Healing*.

So far, I have confined myself to a bird's eye view of the routine as established in the First or Outer Order of the Golden Dawn. The graduated training of the entire Outer was intended as a preparation for the practical work to be performed in the Inner or Second Order of the Roseae Rubeau et Aureae Crucis. The assignation of personal magical work seems deliberately to have been postponed until after the Vault reception. It was held that the Ceremony formulated a link between the Aspirant and his Augoeides, that connect serving therefore as a guide and a powerful protection which is clearly required in the works of Ceremonial Magic. Since at the commencement of each serious operation the Initiate must needs exalt himself towards his higher and divine Genius that through him may flow the divine power which alone is capable of producing a pure magical work, the initial forging of that link is a matter of supreme importance.

Let me now detail the curriculum of work prescribed in the Second Order. The training of the Adeptus Minor consisted of eight separate items, and I quote the following from a syllabus "A–General Orders," now in circulation.

"*Part One. A. Preliminary.* Receive and copy: Notes on the Obligation. The Ritual of the ⑤=⑥ Grade. The manuscript, Sigils from the Rose. The Minutum Mundum. Having made your copies of these and returned the originals you should study them in order also arrange with the Adept in whose charge you are, about your examination in the Temple on the practical work."

"*Part Two*. Receive the Rituals of the Pentagram and Hexagram. Copy and learn them. You can now sit for the written examination in these subjects and complete 'A' by arranging to be tested in your practical knowledge in the Temple.

"*Part One. B. Implements*. Receive the Rituals of the Lotus Wand, Rose-Cross, Sword, and the Elemental Weapons. Copy and return them. There is a written examination on the above subjects–that is on the construction, symbolism, and use of these objects, and the general nature of a consecration ceremony and the forming of invocations. This can be taken before the practical work of making is begun or at any stage during it.

"*Part Two*. This consists in the making of the Implements which must be passed as suitable before the consecration is arranged for, in the presence of a Chief or other qualified Adept. The making and consecration are done in the order given above unless it is preferred to do all the practical work first, and make arrangements for consecration as convenient.

"*Part One. G. Neophyte Formulae*. Receive and copy Z.1. on the symbols and formulae of the Neophyte in this Ceremony. Copy the God-form designs of the Neophyte Ritual. The written examination on the Z. manuscripts may now be taken.

"*Part Two*. To describe to the Chief or other suitable Adept in the Temple the arrangement of the Astral Temple and the relative position of the Forms in it. To build up any God-form required, using the correct Coptic Name."

The above three sections, A. B. G., completed the course prescribed for the Zelator Adeptus Minor, the first sub-grade. The passing of these examinations, conferred the qualification for holding the office of Hierophant, that is the initiator, in the Outer Order of the G. D.

"*Part One. C. Psychic.* This consists in a written examination in the Tatwa system. Its method of use, and an account of any one vision you have had from any card.

"*Part Two.* This consists in making a set of Tatwa cards, if you have not already done so, and sending them to be passed by the Chief or other Adept appointed. To take the examiner on a Tatwic journey, instructing him as if he were a student and vibrating the proper names for a selected symbol.

"*Part One. D. Divination.* Receive and study the Tarot system, making notes of the principal attributions of the Inner method.

"*Part Two. Practical.* On a selected question, either your own, or the examiner's, to work out a Divination first by Geomancy, then by Horary Astrology, then by the complete inner Tarot system, and send in a correlated account of the result.

"*Part One F. Angelic Tablets.* Receive and make copies of the Enochian Tablets, the Ritual of the Concourse of the Forces, and the Ritual of the making of the Pyramid, Sphinx, and God-form for any square. A written examination on these subjects may now be taken.

"*Part Two.* Make and colour a pyramid for a selected square, and to make the God-form and Sphinx suitable to it, and to have this passed by an Adept. To prepare a Ritual for practical use with this square, and in the presence of a Chief or other Adept appointed to build it up astrally and describe the vision produced. To study and play Enochian chess, and to make one of the Chess boards and a set of Chessmen.

"*Part One. E. Talismans.* Receive a manuscript on the making and consecrating of Talismans. Gather Names, Sigils, etc., for a Talisman for a special purpose. Make a design for both designs of it and send it in for a Chief to pass. Make up a special ritual for consecration to the purpose you have in mind and arrange a time with the Chief for the Ceremony of Consecration.

"*H. Consecration and Evocation.* Subject: A ceremony on the formulae of Ritual Z. 2. Must be prepared before Examiner and must meet with his approval as to method, execution and effect."

In the early Temples there was also an issued catalogue of manuscripts, enumerating in alphabetical order the documents circulated amongst the Zelatores Adepti Minores.

A. General Orders. The Curriculum of Work prescribed.
B. The Lesser and Supreme Rituals of the Pentagram.
C. The Rituals of the Hexagram.
D. Description of Lotus Wand, and Ritual of Consecration.
E. Description of Rose Cross and the Ritual of Consecration.
F. Sigils from the Rose.
G. Sword and Four Implements, with Consecration Ritual.
H. Clavicula Tabularum Enochi.
J. Notes on the Obligation of the Adeptus Minor.
K. Consecration Ceremony of the Vault.
L. History Lecture.
M. Hermes Vision, and Lineal Figures of the Sephiroth.
N. O. P. Q. R. Complete Treatise on the Tarot, with Star Maps.
S. The Attributions of the Enochian Tablets.
T. The Book of The Angelical Keys or Calls.
U. Lecture on Man, the Microcosm.
W. Hodos Chamelionis, the Minutum Mundum.
X. The Egyptian God-forms as applied to the Enochian Squares.
Y. Enochian Chess.
Z. Symbolism of the Temple, Candidate, and Ritual of the Neophyte grade.

All the documents from A to Z listed above will be found reproduced in these volumes, though I have not retained that particular order. The sole omissions are the documents lettered H. J., L. and part of M.

"J" consists simply of an elaborated commentary upon the Adeptus Minor Obligation, written in a florid ponderous style reminiscent of Eliphas Levi-cum-Arthure Edward Waite.

"H" Clavicula Tabularum Enochi, is a more or less lengthy manuscript, turgid and archaic, for the most part repeating, though not clearly, the contents of "S, The Book of Concourse of the Forces." Incidentally, this document is practically a verbatim duplicate of part of a lengthy manuscript to be found in the Manuscript Library of the British Museum, Sloane 307. A good deal of the advice given is typically mediaeval, and definitely unsound from a spiritual viewpoint, and is certainly not in accord with the general lofty tenor of the remaining Order teaching. It explains how to find precious metals and hidden treasure, and how to drive away the elemental guardians thereof. It is an inferior piece of work–as also is the document "L", and so I have decided to omit both.

"M" has two sections, the Hermes Vision which I do propose to give, and the Lineal Figures of the Sephiroth. Because of the extreme complexity of the latter, and because it will be impossible to reproduce the several geometrical drawings in colour which accompany that manuscript, the writer has deemed it sufficient to restate it in a general manner as a note to the instruction on Telesmatic Images.

The whole of the above described material I have arranged and classified in an entirely different way. The contents of these volumes will be found divided up into so many chapters or separate books, each complete by itself. And the material in each book will be seen to be consistent and appertain to parts of the magical technique which are placed with it. The Table of Contents describes my method of arrangement.

Clearly from these disclosures there may be drastic results. But the good, I trust, will immeasurably and ultimately outweigh whatever evil may come. That some careless people will hurt themselves and burn their fingers experimenting with matters not wholly understood seems almost inevitable. Theirs, however, will be the fault. For the formulae of Magic require intensive study prior to experimental work. And since all the important formulae are given in their entirety, and nothing withheld that is of the least value, there should be no excuse for anybody harming himself. No serious hurt should come to anyone. On the contrary, the gain to those serious students of Magic and Mysticism who have initiative and yet refuse to involve themselves with corrupt occult orders, and it is to these that I fain would speak, should be immeasurable.

You are being given a complete system of attainment. This you must study and develop at your own leisure, applying it in your own particular way. The system is complete and effectual, as well as noble. The grade rituals as I shall reproduce them have been tampered with, in some cases unintelligently. Their efficacy, however, is not impaired, for the principal portion of those grade rituals, which teaches the art of invocation, is intact. So that the unwise editing that they have received in the past several years has not actually damaged them; all that has been removed are a few items, more or less important, of Qabalistic knowledge. If the reader feels that these might be value to him, and for the sake of tolerable completeness would like to have them, by studying such Qabalistic texts as the *Zohar* and the *Sepher Yetzirah* both of which are now in English translation, or some such work as Waite's *Holy Kaballah*, he will be in possession of the fundamental facts. It is in other parts of the Order work in injudicious tampering has been at work. Most of this is now restored and I believe that this book is an accurate representation of the whole of the Order work from Neophyte to Theoricus Adeptus Minor.

Some portions of the manuscripts have required editing, principally from the literary point of view. Whole paragraphs have had to be deleted, others shortened, sentences made more clear, the redundant use of many words eliminated, and a general coordination of the manuscripts undertaken. Certain other sections–have been completely rewritten to render them more coherent. But nothing that is essential or vital to the magical tenor or understanding of any document will be omitted, changed or altered. This I avow and publicly swear. Where personally I have seen fit to make comment on any matter in order to clarify the issue or to indicate its antecedents, or connections in other parts of the work, that comment or remark is so marked by me with initials.

Let me therefore urge upon the sincere reader whose wish it is to study this magical system, to pay great attention to the scheme of the grade rituals, to obtain a bird's eye view of the whole, to study every point, its movement and teaching. This should be repeated again and again, until the mind moves easily from one point of the ritual to another. The synthetic outline of those rituals presented in this Introduction should be found helpful as assisting in this task. Let him also study the diagrams of the Temple lay-out, and build up in his imagination a clear and vivid picture of that Temple together with the appropriate officers and their movements. Then it will be an easy matter to devise a simple form of self-initiation. It will be simple to adapt the text to solo performance. But a careful scrutiny and examination of the entire system should long precede any effort to do practical work, if serious harm and danger is to be avoided. The language needs first of all to be mastered, and the symbolic ideas of the whole system assimilated and incorporated into the very fibre of one's being. Intellectual acquaintance with every aspect of the subject is just as necessary as personal integrity and selfless devotion to an ideal. Sincerity is indeed the most trustworthy shield and buckler that any student may possess, but if he neglects the intellectual mastery of the subject, he will soon discover where his heel of Achilles is located. But these two combined are the only safeguards, the fundamental requisites to an insight into the significance of Magic. Not only are they the only sure foundation, but they conduce to the continual recollection of the goal at the end, which understanding arises through penetrating to the root of the matter, without which the student may stray but too readily from the narrow way stretching before him. No matter how brilliant his intellectual capacity, no matter how ardent his sincerity or potent his dormant magical power, always must he remember that they matter absolutely in no way unless applied to the Great Work–the knowledge and conversation of the Higher and Divine Genius. "Power without wisdom," said a poet, "is the name of Death." And as Frater D. D. C. F. so rightly said of one phase of magical work, but which has its application to the whole scheme, "Know thou that this is not to be done lightly for thine amusement or experiment, seeing that the forces of Nature were not created to be thy plaything or toy. Unless thou doest thy practical magical works with solemnity, ceremony and reverence, thou shalt be like an infant playing with fire, and thou shalt bring destruction upon thyself." In deviation from these injunctions lie the only actual dangers in the divine science.

One of the essentials of preliminary work, is the committing to memory of the important correspondences and attributions. And I cannot insist too strongly that this is fundamental. The student must make himself familiar first of all with the Hebrew Alphabet, and learn how to write the names of the Sephiroth and Deity Names in that tongue–he will realise their value when he approaches the practical work of invocation. Much time should be spent studying and meditating upon the glyph of the Tree of

Life and memorising all the important attributions–divine Names, names of Archangels, Angels and Spheres and elements. All the symbols referred to the lamens of the officers should be carefully meditated upon, as also the various admission badges, and other symbols given in the knowledge lectures. Above all, a great deal of time and attention should be paid to the Middle Pillar technique and the Vibratory Formulae of divine names.

The student can easily adapt any fair-sized room to the exigencies of a Temple. The writer has worked in one hardly larger than a long cupboard, about ten feet long by six or seven wide. All furniture from the centre should be cleared away, leaving a central space in which one may freely move and work. A small table covered with a black cloth will suffice for the Altar, and the two Pillars may be dispensed with but formulated in the imagination as present. He may find it very useful to paint flashing Angelic Tablets according to the instructions found elsewhere, as well as the Banners of the East and West, placing these in the appropriate cardinal quarters of his improvised Temple. If he is able to obtain small plaster-casts of the heads of the Kerubim–the lion, the eagle, bull and man–and place these in the proper stations, they will be found together with the Tablets to impart a considerable amount of magical vitality and atmosphere to the Temple. What actually they do bestow is rather subtle, and perhaps indefinable. They are not absolute essentials, however, and may be dispensed with. But since Magic works by the intervention of symbol and emblem, the surrounding of the student's sphere with the correct forms of magical symbolism, assists in the impressing of those symbols within the aura or sphere of sensation, the true magical Temple. This may be left to the ingenium and the convenience of the student himself to discover after having made a close examination of the documents involved.

Another matter upon which brief comment must be made concerns the Instruments. It would have given me great pleasure to have had illustrations of these reproduced in colour, for only thus can one appreciate their significance and the part they play in ceremonial. But this unfortunately has not been possible. Thus they are given only in black and white, which obviously cannot impart anything but the merest fraction of their actual beauty and suggestiveness. And I impress upon the serious student, even implore him, to betake upon himself the trouble of making these instruments himself. They are very simple to fashion. And the results obtained, to say little of the knowledge acquired or the intuitive processes that somehow are stimulated by that effort, are well worth even a great deal of bother. To adopt temporarily part of the terminology now current among analytical psychologists, and identifying the latent spiritual self of man with what is known as the Unconscious, then be it remembered that this vast subterranean stream of vitality and memory and inspiration can only be reached by means of a symbol. For the latter, states Jung, "is the primitive expression of the Unconscious, while on the other hand it is an idea corresponding to the highest intuition produced by consciousness." Thus these weapons and magical instruments are symbolic representations of psychic events, of forces inhering within the potentiality of the inner man. By means of their personal manufacture, magical consecration and continual employment they may be made to affect and stimulate the dormant side of man's nature. It is an interesting fact that in his practice, Jung encouraged his patients to pain symbolic designs which sometimes were comparable to the Eastern mandalas. It seems that the effort to paint these designs had the effect of straightening out stresses and knots in the unconscious, thus accomplishing the therapeutic object of the analysis. And not only were they thus means of self-expression but these designs produced a counter-effect of fascinating, healing and stimulating a renewed activity the hitherto unmanifested psyche.

With the exception that the ordinary magical student is not neurotic or psychopathic, the techniques are rather similar. For the magical tradition has always insisted upon the routine to be followed by the aspirant to that art. He was required to fashion the implements himself, and the more laborious he found that task, with the greater difficulties thrown before him, by so much more were those efforts of spiritual value. For not only are these instruments symbols or expressions of inner realities, but what is infinitely more of practical worth, their actual projection in this way from within outwards, the physical fashioning and painting of these instruments, also works an effect. They bring to life the man that was asleep. They react upon their maker. They become powerful magical agents, true talismans of power.

Thus, the Lotus Wand is declared in the Ritual to have the colours of the twelve signs of the Zodiac painted on its stem, and it is surmounted by the Lotus flower of Isis. It symbolises the development of creation. The Wand has ever been a symbol of the magical Will, the power of the spirit in action. And its description in the instruction on the Lotus Wand is such that it is seen to embrace the whole of nature–the Sephiroth, the spiritual aspects of the elements, and the action of the Sun upon all life by a differentiating process. Even as the whole of nature is the embodiment of a dynamic will, the visible form and vehicle of a spiritual consciousness. The Lotus flower grows from the darkness and gloom of the secret depths, through the waters, ever striving to open its blossoms on the surface of the waters to the rays of light of the Sun. So is the true magical or spiritual will secreted within the hidden depths of the soul of man. Unseen, sometimes unknown and unsuspected, it lies latent through the whole of the life. By these rites of Magic, its symbols and exercises, we are enabled to assist its growth and development, by piercing through the outer husks of the restricting shell, until it bursts into full bloom–the flower of the human spirit, the Lotus of the higher Soul. "Look for the flower to bloom in the silence...It shall grow, it will shoot up, it will make branches and leaves and form buds while the storm continues, while the battle lasts...It is the flower of the soul that has opened." Note, moreover, the description of and the comment made by Jung to a symbolic design brought to him by one of his patients, evidently a design like to the Lotus Wand, for he says: "The plant is frequently a structure in brilliant fiery colours and is shown growing out of a bed of darkness and carrying the blossom of light at the top, a symbol similar to the Christmas tree." This is highly suggestive, and students both of Yoga and Magic will find in this curious indications of the universality of cogent symbols. Magical processes and symbols are, in short, receiving confirmation at the hands of experimental psychology. It remains at the hands of experimental psychology. It remains for the reader to benefit thereby.

The Rose-Cross is a Lamen or badge synthesising a vast concourse of ideas, representing in a single emblem the Great Work itself–the harmonious reconciliation in one symbol of diverse and apparently contradictory concepts, the reconciliation of divinity and manhood. It is a highly important symbol to be worn over the heart during every important operations. It is a glyph, in one sense, of the higher Genius to whose knowledge and conversation the student is eternally aspiring. In the Rituals it is described as the Key of Sigils and Rituals.

The Sword is a weapon symbolising the critical dispersive faculty of the mind. It is used where force and strength are required, more particularly for banishing than for invoking–as though conscious intellection were allied to the power of Will. When employed in certain magical ceremonies with the point upwards, its nature magical ceremonies with the point upwards, its nature is transformed into an instrument similar to the Wand. The Elemental weapons of the Wand, Cup, Dagger, and Pentacle are symbolical representations of the forces employed for the manifestation of the inner self, the elements required for the incarnation of the divine. They are attributed to the four letters of Tetragrammaton. All of these are worth making, and by creating them and continually employing them intelligently in the ways shown by the various rituals, the student will find a new power developing within him, a new centre of life building itself up from within.

One last word of caution. Let me warn the student against attempting difficult and complex ceremonies before he has mastered the more simple ones. The syllabus provided on a former page for the use of the Minor Adept grades the work rather well. The consecration ceremonies for the magical implements are, of their kind, excellent examples of ceremonial work. Classical in nature, they are simple in structure and operation, and provide a harmonious and easily flowing ritual. A good deal of experience should be obtained with the constant use of these and similar types which the student should himself construct along these lines. A variety of things may occur to his mind for which a variety of operations may be performed. This of course, applies only to that phase of his studies when the preliminary correspondences and attributions have been thoroughly memorised and what is more, understood, and when the meditations have been performed. This likewise is another matter have been performed. This likewise is another matter upon which too much emphasis cannot be laid.

Above all, the Pentagram and Hexagram rituals should be committed to memory so that no effort is required to recall at a moment's notice the points or angles of these figures from which the invocation of a certain force commences. Short ceremonies should be devised having as their object the frequent use of these lineal figures so that they become a part of the very manner in which the mind works during ceremonial. After some time has elapsed, and after considerable experience with the more simple consecration formulae, the student feeling more confident of himself and his ritualistic capacity, let him turn to the complex ceremonies whose formulae are summarised in the manuscripts Z. 2. These require much preparation, intensive study, and a great deal of rehearsal and experience. Moreover, he must not be disappointed if, at first, the results fall short of his anticipations. Persistence is an admirable and necessary virtue, particularly in Magic. And let him endeavor to penetrate into the reasons for the apparent worthlessness or puerility of the aims of these formulae, such as transformation, evocation, invisibility, by reflection on the spiritual forces which must flow through him in order to effect such ends. And let him beware of the booby trap which was set up in the Order–of doing but one of these ceremonies, or superficially employing any phase of the system as though to pass an examination, and considering in consequence that he is the master of the technique.

My work is done.

"Let us work, therefore, my brethren and effect righteousness, because the Night cometh when no man shall labour…May the Light which is behind the veil shine through you from your throne in the East on the Fratres and Sorores of the Order and lead them to the perfect day, when the glory of this world passes and a great light shines over the splendid sea."

The Complete Golden Dawn System of Magic
Copyright 1984 - New Falcon Publications

Volume One
THE MAGICAL ALPHABET
INTRODUCTION

One of my preoccupations over the last fifty years, ever since I have been actively involved in the study as well as the dissemination of the basic principles of Magic, Qabalah and Occultism in general, is the discrepancy between what the system teaches and the character structure of the average student and even leaders of the occult groups. For awhile it created a good deal of anxiety simply because it appeared to me that there should be some degree of coincidence between student and system.

It was not until many years afterwards that I came to be aware of the function of therapy. At that time I had some dear friends who had amongst their acquaintances some psychotherapists in London where I then resided. Some of them I met socially when we discussed this particular problem that was haunting me. A few agreed with me that there was only one remedy for this discrepancy and that was to enter therapy as a patient. I did this, remaining in therapy for several years and I must say it benefited me enormously. Even today, three or four decades later I still get an occasional letter from a student here, there and anywhere making the statement that I seem to be one of the few sane writers on the subject. True or not, they perceive that there is a difference in one who has had therapy and another who has not.

Today therefore I am adamant both to correspondents and visitors alike that to obtain the greatest benefit from Magic which is as it were a post-graduate study there should be some undergraduate work in personal therapy. The dividends are enormous.

For a long while it seemed to me that Jungian therapy provided the answer to this problem. However from time to time I would meet or hear from a correspondent who complained that that form of therapy was like Ain Soph, without end. So I have concluded that Jungian analysis can be likened to herpes genitalis, that is it is forever. This has resulted finally in entertaining serious doubts about the efficacy of Jung's system as a therapy; as a philosophy I have little quibble, even if many authorities in the occult field that this is the only form of spiritual therapy. Of course this is nonsense. In therapy one is not concerned whether its contents are spiritual or otherwise, but whether it enables one to face and deal with one's own latent infantility which is eternally getting in the way. Whether magical or occult authorities like it or not Freudian analysis is infinitely more effective.

Out of the Freudian school there has evolved an entirely new and different approach to this problem which curiously enough, though it makes no claim in this direction, is far more spiritual in its effects and its results than anything else I know. Wilhelm Reich, originally an ardent disciple of Freud, developed a system of therapy which astonishingly enough is a bridge from orthodox psychotherapy to the occult world. He himself would never have admitted this. And in fact he would rather have died than recognize this, but facts are facts which cannot be denied. My experience as a psychotherapist extending over some thirty years or more, has surprised me in the discovery that many patients who prior to therapy had no talent for Magic etc., found themselves profoundly involved in what might be called mystical or religious experiences on the couch at the end of the session. Therefore after all these many years I still insist that the student of this subject involve himself deeply in therapy but nowadays I make the proviso that it be a form of Reichian or neo-Reichian therapy. A great deal of time, money and heartache will be spared the student if, when he decides to follow my counsel, he attempts to seek out a therapist or teacher who is trained in these techniques. Admittedly there are problems in this direction but these are not insurmountable. Any student anywhere in this country desirous of following my counsel but is unable to find an adequate therapist is invited to do one of two things. First to write to me directly in care of my publishers Falcon Press in Phoenix. I promise to reply at once, giving counsel on whom they should consult. Second, write to my friend and colleague Christopher Hyatt, also care of Falcon Press for further advice. He is not only a first rate therapist himself with extensive training in both experimental and psychoanalytic therapy but is at the same time a very perceptive and intuitive therapist and teacher of many years experience. In addition Hyatt has a strong background in occult subjects, particularly with meditative and Eastern techniques. This with his Western knowledge makes him an ideal choice for those students seriously involved with the occult. At the very least if he is not personally available he too can make recommendations to other practitioners in the field.

In other places I have dogmatically stated that the Golden Dawn as a functioning occult Order has been defunct for years. It gives me pleasure to state that in the past several years a new group of young student have attempted to formulate actively functioning Temples employing the traditional techniques. There are now a few Temples scattered throughout the country to which I would be glad to refer the interested student.

The Hermetic Order of the Golden Dawn issued its own account of its history. It claimed to be "an Hermetic Society whose members are taught the principles of occult science and the Magic of Hermes. During the early part of the last century, several prominent Adepti and Chiefs of the Order in France and England died, and their death caused a temporary dormant condition of Temple work." It goes on to state that these adepts "received indeed and have handed down to us their doctrine and system of Theosophy and Hermetic Science and the higher Alchemy from a long series of practical investigators whose origin is traced to the Fratres Roseae Crucis of Germany, which association was founded by one Christian Rosenkreutz about the year 1398 A.D....

"The Rosicrucian revival of Mysticism was but a new development of the vastly older wisdom of the Qabalistic Rabbis and of that very ancient secret knowledge, the Magic of the Egyptians, in which the Hebrew Pentateuch tells you that Moses, the founder of the Jewish system, was 'learned', that is, in which he had been initiated.

This is the Golden Dawn historical claim. Many have questioned its veracity. That really does not concern us at this moment. Perhaps by far the best and most objective account of its history, short and concise, was written by Aleister Crowley in *Liber LXI vel Causae*. The first few paragraphs are so well stated as to warrant quotation here:

"Some years ago a number of cipher MSS. were discovered and deciphered by certain students. They attracted much attention, as they purported to derive from the Rosicrucians. You will readily understand that the genuineness of the claim matter no whit, such literature being judged by itself, not by its reputed sources.

"Among the MSS was one which gave the address of a certain person in Germany, who is known to us as S.D.A. Those who discovered the ciphers wrote to S.D.A., and in accordance with instructions received, an Order was founded which worked in a semi-secret manner.

"After some time S.D.A. died; further requests for help were met with a prompt refusal from the colleagues of S.D.A. It was written by one of them that S.D.A.'s scheme had always been regarded with disapproval. But since the absolute rule of the adepts is never to interfere with the judgments of any other person whomsoever–how much more, then, one of themselves, and that one most highly revered!–they had refrained from active opposition. The adept who wrote this added that the Order had already quite enough knowledge to enable it or its members to formulate a magical link with the adepts.

"Shortly after this, one called S.R.M.D. announced that he had formulated such a link, and that himself with two others was to govern the Order."

There is another source of historical material in a small pamphlet written by Dr. W. W. Westcott, in which it is stated that "In 1887 by the permission of S.D.A., a continental Rosicrucian Adept, the Isis-Urania Temple of Hermetic students of the Golden Dawn was formed to give instructions in the mediaeval occult sciences. Fratres M.E.V. with S.A. and S.R.M.D. became the Chiefs, and the latter wrote the rituals in modern English from old Rosicrucian manuscripts (the property of S.A.) supplemented by his own literary researches."

These several statements then give the beginning of the Hermetic Order of the Golden Dawn. Since its inception in the last quarter of the nineteenth century it has exerted far greater influence on the growth and dissemination of practical occult information and knowledge than can be realized by most present day students. At first its membership was recruited from a broad spectrum of English intellectuals and artists and even the clergy, but later came to include quite ordinary men and women from every segment of society and life.

In accord with the spirit of the times, it cloaked itself in a glamour of mystery and secrecy. Regardless of the various rumors that circulated about it, it came to be very difficult to join this Order. Even A. E. Waite, who some regard as an occult authority, sarcastically remarked in his autobiography that his application was black-balled. It was after a period of time that he reapplied at the urging of some of his friends and only then was he accepted.

Its teachings and methods of instruction were surrounded by oaths and various penalties attached to the most awe inspiring ritual-obligations to ensure secrecy. You will see what these are in various rituals that are given in the body of the text. It is now common knowledge that Arthur Machen, Florence Farr, W. B. Yeats, Algernon Blackwood, Aleister Crowley, Dion Fortune, and A. E. Waite–to mention only a few–were members of this prestigious organisation. It should be self-evident then that some of its members were not the usual flakey nit-wits some critics are disposed to believe, but prominent and intelligent people.

Perhaps some attention should be given to the secular names of some of those whose Order mottoes have been given above. Sapere Aude and Non Omnis Morjar were the mottoes chosen by Dr. William W. Westcott, a London physician and a coroner by occupation. M.E.V., or Magnum est Veritas was the motto of Dr. William R. Woodman, an eminent Freemason of the last century, who died in 1891 very shortly after the Order was founded and therefore did not play much of active role in its governance. S.R.M.D. or S. Rhiogail Ma Dhream, the motto of Samuel Liddell Mathers also known as McGregor Mathers, was the most active of the chiefs of the Order. He also used the motto Deo Duce Comit

Ferro. He has been described at some length in a biographical study *The Sword of Wisdom* by Ithel Colquhoun, well worth reading in this connection.

Westcott was the author of a couple of minor little books and the editor of an hermetic and alchemical series of writings, well prized today. He was prominent in certain Masonic circles of the day.

Mathers was the translator of three mediaeval magical texts. *The Greater key of King Solomon, The Book of the Sacred Magic of Abramelin the Mage*, and *The Kaballah Unveiled* (which consisted of certain portions from Knorr von Rosenroth's Latin rendition of parts of the Zohar–more distinguished however by a relatively long introduction of considerable erudition and which well warrants republication by itself as an introduction to the study of the Qabalah.)

In this connection I would like to recommend *The Rosy Cross Unveiled* by Christopher McIntosh, which purports to give a history, mythology and the rituals of an occult order (published by Aquarian Press Ltd. 1980).

In as much as both Mathers and Westcott had dual mottoes, it should be remarked that one was for use in the Outer Order of the Golden Dawn, the other being reserved of the Inner Order of the R.R. et A.C.

S.D.A. was the abbreviation of the motto Sapiens Dominabitur Astris chosen by a Fraulein Anna Sprengel of Nuremberg. Though polemics are outside the scope of this introduction, in all fairness to the enquiring student I should mention a highly critical and destructive study of the Order entitled *The Magicians of the Golden Dawn* by Ellic Howe. It is mentioned here because amidst all of its prejudicial criticism while is not difficult to demolish, there is some significant historical data of considerable value.

There is also, I should mention, my own account of the Golden Dawn history at some length–*What You Should Know About the Golden Dawn* (Falcon Press, Phoenix, Arizona, 1983). In addition to tracing some of the obscurities relating to the origins of the Order, it provides a bird's eye view of its teachings that might be of value to the current reader. The Order provided initiation into the Mysteries in a highly organized and systematic manner.

INITIATION

Initiation is the preparation for immortality. Man is only potentially immortal. Immortality is acquired when the purely human part of him becomes allied to that spiritual essence which was never created, was never born, and shall never die. It is to effect this spiritual bond with the highest, that the Golden Dawn owes all its rituals and practical magical work.

Initiation means to begin, to start something new. It represents the beginning of a new life dedicated to an entirely different set of principles from those of what Wilhelm Reich once contemptuously termed "homo normalis." With the enormous development of scientific pragmatism, it is conceivable that sometime in the near or distant future, robots or computers will be invented that will, to all intents and purposes, free man from the daily drudgery of common toil. If and when that occurs, what will the average man do with his leisure time? Despite the claims of various protagonists of the free future of man, I doubt that many will turn their time and energy to the pursuit of the Great Work in any of its forms. Most of them will continue to hunt, fish, travel in recreation vehicles, drink beer and grow fat, watch television more and more, concentrate on spectator sports, and continue to their lives on a thoroughly prosaic and mundane level. If there are excursion into outer space, in a view of setting up colonies outside of the earth, I am far from certain that the same fate will not await them as it did all ventures into utopian communities. There are only a mere handful who can tolerate more than a glancing casual look at than the superficial aspects of what life presents to them.

For this handful, the Golden Dawn system presents itself as the answer to their innumerable questions. The system itself is timeless. It did not owe it origins to the formation of that particular Order called the Golden Dawn in the latter part of 19th century. The greater part of it, in one form or another, has existed for centuries–actually forever–not necessarily in the open where it could be attacked by secular and ecclesiastical authorities, but under cover, secretly and safely. Those who were in need of its teachings and work would inevitable be attracted to some one or other of its members, and undergo initiation. This process occurred in the past even as it does today. When the time comes for the inner awakening, as it may be called, all sorts of synchronicities, as Jung might call them, occur which lead them inevitably in the right direction, to the Western Esoteric Tradition.

THE WESTERN ESOTERIC TRADITION

There are a many legends circulating within the occult field that may clarify what is commonly called the Western esoteric tradition as being opposed to the so-called Eastern tradition.

It is held that several centuries ago a group of wise men gathered in the Near East to discuss ways and means of disseminating the ageless wisdom so that no opposition from vested interests would be encountered, and at the same time evoke recognition from those who had evolved to a state of psycho-spiritual "readiness". After much discussion, it was agreed that they should devise a set of pictures that could be circulated as playing cards. Pictures that would tell a story relative to man, and who he was, as well as where he came from. Pictures that would relate him as a person to the greater world in which he found himself. In a word, the Tarot cards came into being a serve such ends. Originally employed as playing cards or for fortune telling, they were carried all over the Near East and Europe by gypsies and other travelling bodies, and eventually permeated all civilized countries in the Western hemisphere.

The other legend is to be found in a document circulated early in the 17th century, the *Fama Fraternatitas*. It purports to narrate the history of one Christian Rosenkreutz, a young man who was educated in one of the monasteries in Germany. He wandered to North Africa and the Near East where he was well received by the wise men resident there. They taught him Alchemy, Astrology and Qabalah, together with other occult subjects. When he left he had acquired a liberal education in the occult arts which he took with him to Germany, to the monastery from which he originally came. Gradually he conveyed his knowledge to a monk here and there, until there were enough more or less enlightened monks to comprise an organizational body that came to be known as the Rosicrucians.

A great deal of the above is legend. Many modern authorities insist that that is all it is–a legend. This runs counter to some of the more common pseudo-Rosicrucian orders of today that claim an impossible antecedent for their own group. Be that as it may, the legend itself gives evidence to the belief that there was a definite body of occult knowledge in existence which could be and was communicated in an order manner.

A third factor that should never be overlooked, but which often is, relates to the nature of the monasteries in Roman Catholic Europe. These were the primary centers of learning in an otherwise ignorant world–the Europe of the dark days. They kept alive the learning of every kind then known, and passed it on faithfully to succeeding generations. We know that many of the faithful studied and practiced both alchemy and astrology. It is also known that the Qabalah of the Hebrews was also studied, even though the motive exoterically seemed to be that it was a valuable tool with which to convert the unhappy Jews to the joys and blessings of Christendom.

The Catholic Church, and also the Church of the Byzantium, has a glorious history of great mystics, of men and women to whom the highest vocation called, the quest for God. There were teachers of mystical meditation and interior prayer in many of the monasteries so that the proper preparation for such a high calling would not be lost. They were of many persuasions, these teachers, and so were the mystics who came out of these institutions. They have left their mark on the Church, despite its apparent antagonism to mysticism as such, due to fear it might challenge the Church's demand for conformity to fixed inherited dogma.

There is another most interesting set of circumstances too often glossed over or not well understood. It relates to one of the most crucial and interesting periods of European history. At one time, it must be recalled that the Arabs had invaded Europe and had virtually conquered a part, if not all of Spain. They brought with them not merely a victorious army, but Islamic cultures as well. That included not solely mathematics, though it is well to reflect on what this one item did to European knowledge, but in addition the Greek classics and literature, from Aristotle on. Their contribution included alchemy as well, astrology and the other occult arts. Above all it brought Islamic mysticism, Sufiism. It flourished not merely in North Africa but in Spain as well. From there it was carried by one means or another to all parts of Europe and to every center of learning.

Simultaneously, Christian mysticism was flourishing in Spain and Europe, and some great and wonderful people were active spreading mystical knowledge far and wide. It was a period of rejuvenation and spiritual growth for Spain and for the Church as a whole.

Furthermore, what must not be forgotten was that a favorable climate was also being evolved for the wandering and exiled Jewish people to flourish in. They contributed enormously to Spanish culture and scientific knowledge, and at the same time a specific Hebraic mysticism was taking shape and form. This included some of the pre-Zoharic literature, as well as some of the greatest names in Qabalistic history.

777 and Other Qabalistic Writings of Aleister Crowley
Including Gematria & Sepher Sepiroth
Copyright 1973 - Red Wheel/Weiser

INTRODUCTION
By Israel Regardie

This is a unique collection of Qabalistic texts without parallel in the entire history of this vast mystical literature. All of them belong to the very early professional career of Aleister Crowley; that is they were written before he had reached the age of 40 years. As every student of the Crowley corpus of writings should know, however, they were used constantly and continuously by him throughout his lifetime.

In the obscure footnotes to *The Vision and The Voice* (Sangreal Foundation, Dallas, 1972) which I recently edited, it soon became evident that few of those explanatory notes of his would make rhyme or reason to the average student unless he were exceedingly well-grounded in the material and methods delineated in those three books. All three need to be studied assiduously over a long period of time before those footnotes become intelligible to any degree. Or until the intrinsic value of the texts themselves is perceived as being of the purest gold.

The first of these three texts is actually one of the installments from the *Equinox*, the fifth, containing a biographical serial entitled *The Temple of King Solomon*. This serial strove to present a more or less dynamic picture of the personality of Aleister Crowley or Frater Perdurabo, to use his Order name, in the course of his progress along the mystical and magical path. The first few installments were written by one of his major disciples of the first decade of this century, Captain (later General) J. F. C. Fuller. After a while, these two men separated, as narrated in *The Confessions of Aleister Crowley* (Hill & Wang, New York 1970). The result was that Crowley being left in the lurch, as it were, wrote the fifth installment as a kind of filler, enabling him to find time to resume the narrative of his attainment interrupted by Fuller's departure.

The "filler" has nothing to do, in reality, with the biographical narrative. It consisted of a set of Qabalistic and pragmatic notes on Number that Crowley had accumulated over the years, and which he now tied together for this purpose.

It consisted of a study of one phase of the Qabalistic process which is held in rather poor esteem today, mostly–so I believe– because the majority of modern writers have not been able to penetrate its mystery. They cannot cope with it in any way. They regard it, unfortunately, on a par with the common practice of numerology and fortune telling, thus missing the boat entirely.

Gematria, as this process is named, is pronounced as *g'mut'ree'ah*. As a method it reminds me somewhat of the mysteries surrounding the usage of the koan in the Rinzai sect of Zen. It seems at first sight nothing but perfect nonsense, this taking liberties with names and letters and numbers. But in point of fact, just as the koan is a meaningful but not necessarily rational statement made from a mystical level of consciousness, so also it may be used to induce a similar type of illumination in the determined student who uses it. Depending on the spiritual state of the reader, Gematria will be perceived either as nonsense of the most grotesque description, or it will awaken some simulacrum of the mystical state originally experienced by its writer.

If you study Crowley's exposition of the number 418, in this second book *Gematria*, for example, something of this high point of view may be perceived. It was not arbitrarily chosen as an important or significant number for him, or for that matter for anyone else. And so with many other numbers. The method does have a definite sphere of usefulness and a vital place in Qabalistic exegetical process, but it does require to be understood.

Never for one moment suspect Crowley of gullibility or naiveté. It may seem at first sight as if he were. But read the first few pages of the essay on Gematria where you will notice his satire, his ridicule, his humor. This should never be ignored or minimized. He never had difficulty poking fun at himself or the methods he used for different purposes. It saved him from gullibility and credulity, the curse of the average occult student. Some of his conclusions on his numerical manipulations therefore are entitled, as the very least, to some scrutiny and examination, and this in turn may lead to respect.

For example, I have always been profoundly impressed by his handling of the number 913 (*Equinox I*, No. V, p. 107). It is the gematria of *Berashith*, a Hebrew word meaning "the beginning", the first word of the Book of Genesis. He starts with a discussion of the number nine, and reduces it by several brilliant permutations and attributions to one, stating that "the many being but veils of the One; and the course of argument leads one to knowledge and worship of each number in turn." In concluding the lengthy analysis, he does state explicitly that "9 is not equal to 1 for the neophyte. These equivalences are dogmatic, and only true by favour of Him in whom All is Truth."

Any man who can write thus of a subject which is taboo because capable of infinite abuse, and which has earned the contempt of several reasonable students of the mysteries, is worthy of respect and consideration.

Right to the end of his days, Crowley felt that gematria was a most useful tool, and tested many of his theoretical and intuitive findings relative to *The Book of the Law* against the manipulations and inspirations of gematria. I must say that I am in complete accord with him in this respect, as testified to by my earliest piece of writing *A Garden of Pomegranates*, in which there is a chapter on gematria.

The second of these, *Liber 777* has been reprinted several times in recent years. All of the new editions improved on the first one, which is rare nowadays and most expensive, by the inclusion of many short essays and commentaries written at various times of Crowley, and added skillfully by the editor after Crowley's demise in 1947.

This book was first started in 1907 shortly after his return from the China expedition. It is humorously referred to in the second essay in *Konx Om Pax* where there are references to the Table of Correspondences in preparation. In point of fact, these tables of correspondences which comprise *Liber 777* and which were not published until 1909, consist of basic information provided originally, piecemeal, in the knowledge lectures of the Hermetic Order of the Golden Dawn. Predicated on his own further studies and experiences, they were enormously expanded by Crowley so that, at first sight, they bear little resemblance to the fragmented tables in the Golden Dawn.

There is a wealth of valuable material here just waiting to be used. Many writers have done so without due acknowledgment.

The book provides a basic system or method of filing new information on any topic and subject. The filing system is predicated on a mere thirty two categories, the Ten Sephiroth of the Tree of Life, and the twenty two letters of the Hebrew Alphabet. Once this schema is understood, any new set of data of any kind can be referred to it, thus undergoing immediate and spontaneous organization and synthesis within the psyche. True, most of the material relates to comparative religion and mythology, including precious stones, herbs and plants, and a multitude of other matters. Because these comprise the basic notions currently employed, one should not feel limited only to these topics. At one time, I experimented allocating the elements of the atomic scale to this Tree, with some modicum of success. Somewhere along the line, in the course of my travels, this set of attributions has got lost, and I never made another attempt to duplicate it. It is mentioned here, though, in the hope that enterprising students will realize the enormous potentialities which lie ahead when using the Tree of Life in this way.

Liber 777 created a new type of literature when it first appeared. It was the first of its kind, and Crowley deserves credit for that, even if some of the material itself is not original. The concept is, and that is all that matters.

In order to get some theoretical idea of the Qabalah as a philosophical schema, there are some modern books outside the Crowley corpus which could be consulted to considerable advantage.

First of all, there is Dion Fortune's masterpiece *The Mystical Qabalah*, which is similarly based on Golden Dawn material. Its value lies in the manner in which she has considered each item and each detail with an exposition which ties them all together intelligibly.

Parallel to this William Gray's *Ladder of Lights*, which is another elucidation of the Tree from a different viewpoint but equally illuminating. Both of these books are limited however merely to a study of the Ten Sephiroth, the main categories of the Tree. Supplementing these is Gareth Knight's *Practical Course in Qabalistic Symbolism* which extends the scope of the previous two books. By studying these three books, good background material should be provided from which to learn to appreciate the enormously valuable task performed by Crowley in *Liber 777* several decades ago. The student can accept as much or as little of the philosophy described in the above-named books as he wishes. It does not matter, so long as the basic schema is understood and applied to *Liber 777*. I foresee but little difficulty in this task.

The third volume included here is *Sepher Sephiroth*, which means simply the Book of Numbers. It is extrapolated from *Equinox* I, No. 8. Originally, the book was started by Allan Bennett, one of the Golden Dawn adepts who took Crowley under his wing to ground him in the fundamental processes of Magic. Qabalah, and meditation. He must have been a most extraordinary man, for his mark on Crowley proved to be indelible–and there are few for whom this may be said.

Allan left one or two other pieces of writing which Crowley reproduced in one or other of the several volumes of the *Equinox*; they are worthy of being referred to. *A Note on Genesis* is a brilliant piece of exposition of Qabalistic principles demonstrating the whole gamut of Golden Dawn teachings, including some of the Qabalistic methods described here. For this reason alone it should be studied. The other was written after he had abandoned the Order to become a Buddhist monk with the sacramental name of the Bhikkhu Ananda Metteya. It is entitled *The Training of the Mind*, a study of how to acquire skill in meditation, one of the fundamentals of the Buddhist way of life. Both essays show the fine calibre of his mind, demonstrating why Crowley was so profoundly impressed by him. Anyway–this book is due in large measure to his efforts which Crowley continued.

Sepher Sephiroth consists of hundreds of Hebrew words selected from several sources that are listed in the front of the text. Most of the words are from the Old Testament and a couple of non-Zoharic texts translated by McGregor Mathers under the title of *The Kaballah Unveiled*, from the Latin edition of Knorr von Rosenroth. These words were arranged according to their numerical value by Bennett. The process and additional words were continued by Crowley after he had inherited the book from his mentor.

There are some strange gematria combinations to be found there, but it is traditionally assumed that if two words have the same number value, a connection of some kind may be said to exist between them. At first sight, in some instances, no such relationship may be perceived, but if the student persists in his study and meditation, he may come to realize something of the profundities of these subtle connections and associations that are not immediately perceived.

I have taken the liberty of deleting a *Table of Factor* (*Equinox* I, No. 8, p. viii-xv), which in reality has nothing whatsoever to do with *Sepher Sephiroth*.* In my opinion it is one of the occasional examples of Crowley's exhibitionism. Sometimes he just had to demonstrate his erudition. Much the same is true of many numbers in the last few pages of the text, (*Equinox* I, No. 8, p. 68-101) save for a few with their corresponding Hebrew words that could be condensed and brought closer together. These pages are omitted because there are no corresponding Hebrew words listed; for the time being they are just a waste of space and paper.

While it is true that the serious student might study other Qabalistic texts and in the future discover new Hebrew words having a numerical value that corresponds to those that I have just now deleted, nevertheless he could make his own additions to *Sepher Sephiroth*, insert a new string of numbers to make a place for his newly found words. And that is as it should be. There should be nothing fixed or rigid about any of these three books. They can be supplemented and expanded by the explorations of each student, depending on his own judgment and ingenuity. But he must not fall into the pitfall of some modern writers who, having no sympathy or understanding of the process, decry it and declare it of little value in the Qabalistic scheme of things.

*This table is included by the publisher in the third edition, 1975

I am also omitting Crowley's Preface to the book. It is a nasty malicious piece of writing, and does not do justice to the system with which he is dealing. Every so often, Crowley falls from the heights which he has seen, and swallows someone else's folly–someone whom he has had occasion to admire. In this case, Sir Richard Burton, not always a wholly reliable authority–outside of *The Arabian Nights*.

The essay on *Gematria* and *Sepher Sephiroth* should be studied together. Some of the profundities of the first will never be perceived until one has meditated long and often on some of the words analyzed in that essay.

I must confess that every now and again during the course of my life I have experienced a thoroughgoing revulsion to Crowley as a person, resulting in the total rejection and neglect of what he has written.

Days, weeks, months or years may elapse. Then "accidentally" I stumble across something he wrote–such as *Gematria* and become so engrossed and enamored of his ingenuity and inspiration that my revulsion becomes almost immediately transcended. This is probably more true of *Gematria* than either of the other two here included. (I am not making reference to his other later writings or poetry or holy books at this moment. They belong in a class by themselves.) The student who has missed the excitement and inner elevation experienced by Gematria–whether of his own making or merely reading Crowley–has missed a very great deal.

One scholar recently suggested to me in a letter that Crowley's knowledge of Hebrew was most limited. He made a very impressive "showing" only. In some ways, I am inclined to agree. But on the other hand, what little he did know he has used extremely effectively and creatively.

Anyway, he was not a dull bluffer like Arthur Edward Waite who pretended to all sorts of linguistic and scholastic skills he in fact never had. Take for example his book *The Secret Doctrine in Israel*, which is lengthy analysis of the Zohar. That book was not written until after a French translation of the Zohar had been made–and of course long before the English one had appeared. The footnotes bear ample testimony to this conclusion. Yet he pretended years prior to that book that this Latin and Hebrew were more than adequate to the task–though they were not. Even his Latin translations of many alchemical texts were merely good editing jobs, the translators having been, amongst others, some elderly Anglican priests, preferring to remain if not anonymous then in obscurity, who had got mixed up with the Golden Dawn and the occult arts in general. They did the "donkey work" of translating difficult material, but Waite got the glory and the swollen head. Whatever may be said perhaps too much about this– he never stooped quite that low.

All of this makes this book *The Qabalah of Aleister Crowley* of greater interest to the average good student whose Hebrew may be no better or no worse than that of Crowley. It may give him heart to pursue his own personal addenda to those books and become as good a Qabalist as was Crowley.

Finally, let me add that the student should own a good Hebrew-English lexicon. Perhaps one of the best ways of using this is to browse through it at random–casually as it were, and then as his interest and excitement mount, look for certain words deliberately and methodically.

For example. Open the lexicon at random, and on that particular page point carelessly to the first word noticed. Transfer the word and its translation to a sheet of paper, and then work out its gematria. Then turn to Sepher Sephiroth to see if that number and word are represented. If not, add them, using page inserts if necessary. Make special entries of such words. As time proceeds, certain other words will evoke special interest and should be treated in the same manner. Try to follow Crowley's analysis of *Berashith* in the essay *Gematria* as a model for the management of these words, and as the basis for meditation to lead to the highest.

Here are a couple of examples. I opened the lexicon at random and selected two words. A variety of Qabalistic methods may be used to elaborate on them. Practice will produce skill and insight.

The first word selected was one meaning "empty." In Hebrew, it is spelled Nun, Ayin, Vav, Resh. Thus its gematria is: 50, 70, 6, 200 = 326. This is a number that is listed in *Sepher Sephiroth*, and surprisingly is that of *Yeheshuah*, the Redeemer. The word for "vision" also comes within the purview of this number. The lexicon word "empty" may seem a far cry from any of these words just mentioned, but…See what a little meditation can do, after having followed a similar procedure to that used by Crowley relative to *Berashith*.

Another word selected at random is "defect, or want." In Hebrew this is spelled Cheth, Samekh, Resh, Vav, final Nun. It's gematria come to 324 (counting the Nun as 50). This, too, is another number already in *Sepher Sephiroth*. But is worth comparing with the words already given there. "Redness", "darkness", "roaring", etc. All three of these Qabalistic texts must be consulted to make sense of these apparently unrelated words and numbers. The process thus becomes a test for one's Qabalistic knowledge and skill, but more importantly the process becomes a stimulus for the surrender of the mind to the mystical experience in which the One is seen to be All, and visa versa.

There are simply no limits to be set to the applications of these numerical processes. It will take only a little practice and experience for the sincere and ingenious student to become aware of the possibilities inherent in gematria. And he will conclude by developing a fine appreciation for the value–individually and collectively–of these three books assembled for the first time as The Qabalah of Aleister Crowley.

Israel Regardie

PREFACES and FOREWORDS
by Israel Regardie

BOOK 4
By Aleister Crowley
First Published in 1980 by Samuel Weiser, Inc.

PREFACE TO PARTS I & II
By Israel Regardie

These two little books impress me to-day as vigorously as they did over forty years ago when I first read them. They embody simplicity, clarity and profundity in a single package without equal in the literature of the occult.

The first one deals with Yoga. Quietly and methodically, Aleister Crowley sets out to debunk the entire subject by stripping it of the mysterious and the glitter. Soberly, he describes each step as a technique of mental discipline leading to the highest. No phase of the discipline is discussed which he himself had not previously worked with.

Most of his experience with Yoga dates back to 1901. On his way to the Himalayas for mountain-climbing, he stopped over in Ceylon to visit his former magical mentor Allan Bennett. While there, they both settled down to the practice of Yoga under the supervision of Shri Parananda. That first round of Yoga eventuated in Dhyana, an overwhelming interior orgasm of the mind. In later years, he returned to the Yoga disciplines, and it was on the basis of these manifold experiences that the wrote Part I of Book IV. It is still as authoritative to-day as it was years ago–perhaps even more so, when migrant yogis and swamis from the East seem as determined as ever to complicate the issue.

Part II deals with magical symbolism. All the paraphernalia employed in ritual magic are carefully explained in both psychological and mystical terms. Magic itself is not quite so easy to understand as is the purely mental and/or physical technique of Yoga.

During the 1920s, Crowley wrote Part III of Book 4 entitled *Magick in Theory and Practice*, where he again attempted to explore and explain the subject on a more practical level. But Magick requires for its understanding, a thoroughgoing comprehension of this small work Part II of Book 4. In my estimation it is a classic.

Israel Regardie
March 21, 1969
Studio City, Calif.

Magic Without Tears
By Aleister Crowley

PREFACE
By Israel Regardie

When I first read *Magick without Tears* some ten years ago, I confess it left very little impression on me. It seemed long and tedious to say the least. I suppose I was more accustomed to the dazzling pyrotechnics and virtuosity of the earlier Crowley, to *The Equinox*, and other books of sixty years ago. But my reaction was a serious mistake, as I discovered several years later when the opportunity to read it again presented itself. For despite its wit and humor, *Magick without Tears* is a serious, sober and sophisticated piece of good writing. It dazzles, but in a rather more restrained way than his antecedent work. It requires quiet study and sober meditation to appreciate its scholarship, its profound insight and its great worth.

The letters that comprise this volume were written fairly close to the end of Crowley's life here on earth. (It seems difficult at this writing to realize that he was born almost a century ago–in 1875!) Some critics are inclined to believe that he had become feebleminded toward the end, a condition which some felt to be due to the "softening" of his brain through his use of drugs. He was troubled by emphysema it is true, brought about by many years of asthma and heavy smoking. Heroin had long before been prescribed to manage his bronchial asthma and because it was about the only medication that gave him relief, permitting him to breathe with some ease, he eventually became addicted. For the benefit of those who would like to believe that his mental faculties had become impaired, I must assert that these letters give lie to that assumption.

They are incomparably lucid and well organized. Even his apparent rambling (at times) had motives, aimed solely at the elucidation of obscure points of doctrine and teaching. Beyond all other considerations, these letters prove the inherent clarity and inexorable logic of his thinking. It never fails or falters, even for a single moment. General semantics finds its most staunch supporter in the person and writing of Aleister Crowley. There is hardly a page in this book that does not insist that the enquirer clarify her referents. Letter 28 is a splendid example of this insistence. There are pitifully few occult writers that even know what general semantics is all about.

From personal experience of many years ago, I recall that one of his constant companions, almost a bible, was *Skeat's Etymological Dictionary*. Here it is thrust repeatedly under the nose of both the enquirer and the reader. At all times he seeks to know what you mean by the terms you employ in your questions and statements. By the same token, he demands that you expect no less of him. In this respect, if in no other, this book is priceless.

The first few letters with alphabet headings are essentially by way of introduction, setting the pace, as it were, for the later ones. But they are loaded with the most important details concerning the Great Work, his organization of the A∴A∴, and what is expected of the student once he has become a probationer of that Order.

As soon as the chapter letters are reached, however, one is plunged into intellectual and spiritual depths or heights which the author struggles to make reasonably clear. The first letter borrows the axioms, theorems and propositions written for an earlier book, *Magick in Theory and Practice*. They are certainly worth reviewing and contain more than appears at first sight.

The order of the letters does not make for easy reading in the sense of being continuous or consecutive. They could have been rearranged in such a way as to give the reader a more steady and gradual introduction to some highly complex and controversial issues. After due reflection however, I have decided to leave them in their present order, and allow the reader to work out his own approach to their contents. It is suggested that the reader first browse through the book as a whole in order to become familiar with the general nature of the material presented. Do remember that there is a table of contents and an index. Later, the reader could take one letter at a time, dealing with a certain topic, study it, and meditate on whatever sections of that letter seem to warrant it. In this way, I believe, he will obtain a great deal more from this very profound book than if he tried to read it straight though it were a novel, or an otherwise conventional textbook.

Letters (divided here into chapters) 6, 7 and 8 are entitled "The Three Schools of Magick." They were written to expatiate upon a short quotation from *Liber 418: The Vision and the Voice*, a series of transcendental experiences based upon the Enochian system of Magick. Crowley states that they were written by a Mr. Gerard Aumont, and that he is quoting from that long essay.

I met Gerard Aumont late in 1928. He was at that time a French journalist who lived and worked in Tunisia, though he came up to Paris every now and again to meet with Crowley. The entire content of this long essay bears entirely too many distinguishing features of Crowley himself for it to have been penned by anyone other than Crowley. It would appear that Crowley was quite willing to have written essays, etc., and where convenient to use either a pseudonym or to let another party take full credit for the writing.

I state categorically that Aumont was incapable of writing this particular essay. Every phrase, most turns of expression, the very egocentricity of the point of view, the penetrating comprehension of Magick and history, are all Crowley's work and none other. If one has studied the numerous works of Crowley and absorbed the uniqueness of his particular viewpoint, the hand of the master himself will be recognized.

Finally, I doubt whether he would have been willing to quote at such great length from the writing of any other author for these letters. Many short quotations from several writers are certainly to be found in this volume, but not one of such great length.

In a word, Crowley is quoting from himself.

One of Crowley's personal prejudices is highlighted in a curious way in one of these letters. It relates to color. In a quotation from "The Three Schools of Magick" he refers to the stupid attempt by Annie Besant and Bishop. Leadbeater to set up Jiddu Krishnamurti as the World Teacher. Both of these Theosophical leaders had made all sorts of preparation for this event, including the organization of special societies and service groups which would do honor to him. Crowley wrote of it:

> *To make the humiliation more complete, a wretched creature was chosen who, to the most loathsome moral qualities, added the most fatuous imbecility. And then blew up!...We cannot support that humanity is so entirely base as to accept Krishnamurti...*

To this was added a footnote: "This passage was written in 1924 e.v. The Master Therion arose and smote him. What seemed a menace is now hardly a memory."

A more unkind reference could hardly have been made. First of all, Krishnamurti was selected by the two neo-Theosophists while still a minor: on what basis I hardly know. It is quite possible that his boyish vanity may have been flattered by having such fulsome honors and praise heaped upon him. A lengthy reference to this episode was made years earlier in *The Equinox*, Vol I, No. 10. There is a section, *In Memoriam–John Yarker*, the Sovereign Grand Master General of this Rite, who had died on March 20, 1913. The second protested the attendance of an unnamed follower of Leadbeater (though his name is more than hinted at), a follower who

> *is not and never was a member of a lodge in good standing working under a Grand Lodge of Free and Accepted Masons. The Santcuary must be purged...He is not even a free man, but the hired tool of a woman...This woman–pollution to that pure word!–comes to us from the nauseous fraud by which she made herself the real if not the nominal mistress of the T.S.... This is the secret object of the attempt to hold the election of S.G.M.G. without due notice, to drag our holy Rite into the mire, to chain it to the chariot wheels of a Krishnamurti, to make us panders to the antique and impotent uncleanness of senile sodomite.*

Apart from the contempt exuded in this speech, there is an amusing and hypocritical element to be detected here that should not be lost in the shuffle. By his own admission Crowley was, if not an overt homosexual deviant, then a person who had a powerful homosexual component in his character structure. His strictures against Leadbeater as an old sodomite are, to say the least, evidence that he was dishonest and unscrupulous where it suited his purpose regardless of any peculiarities inherent in his own personality. It is the pot calling the kettle black. *The Bagh-i-Muattar*, one of the books Crowley wrote sometime during 1914, is nothing else but a textbook on homosexual and deviant practices hidden under the mask of Sufi mysticism. That is Crowley's business, not mine. But if then he attacks another person on the grounds of homosexuality, his hypocrisy stands out like a sore thumb and will win him but little support.

I hold no brief for Bishop Leadbeater, believe me. My own condemnation of him rests, not on the grounds that he was "an old sod" or a "bugger," but that he, together with Mrs. Besant, was responsible for the thoroughgoing betrayal of the Theosophical movement and for the perversion of Mme. Blavatsky's original teachings.

Crowley has slung the not very salubrious term "nigger" around with far too much carelessness. In one place he has used this word where Krishnamurti is concerned–which is a nasty piece of Anglo-Saxon assumption of superiority–and for the black people in this country. His racist prejudices are far too evident to leave one comfortable.

Following the speech quoted from *The Equinox*, Vol. I, No. 10, there is an account of the legal proceedings in Chingleput, India, where J. Narayaniah was suing Annie Besant to regain custody of his two sons–one of whom was Krishnamurti. Of the latter, the father said: "the boy was not able to write a decent English letter" and so, of course, was incapable of writing the book *At the Feet of the Master* which was said to have been his creation. The father believed, as so many people have since, that it was authored by Leadbeater.

The fact remains that when Krishnamurti came to maturity, he repudiated both Besant and Leadbeater, as well as the various organizations that had been formed to worship him as well as to further his cause as World Teacher. For this alone he commands vast respect, if nothing more. It required great courage to step down voluntarily from a role originally foisted upon him and which he came to realize he was unfit to fulfill. Since that day he has evidenced a loathing for organizations, for societies of the kind of the Theosophical Society, and has espoused a free philosophic attitude that is reminiscent of Zen Buddhism at its best. He has lectured on many occasions throughout the world, and has several books to his credit that have been thought to be both profound and wise. Crowley's condemnation is cruel and harsh, perhaps because of his own ambition to be Logos Aionos, the Word of the Aeon, the World Teacher, and so he was a ruthless competitor who damned all other competition, real or otherwise.

The reader should notice that every letter begins and ends with a formula–two quotations from *The Book of the Law*. Crowley felt compelled to open every letter and indeed every meeting with any individual with these quotations. Bidding adieu was also marked by the same type of gesture. Some people have felt that he made a laughingstock of himself by so doing, but for this kind of reproach he cared nothing. So long as he felt commanded by that book to behave in such a manner he proceeded to do so, come what may. The verses used are "Do what thou wilt shall be the whole of the Law" and "Love is the law, love under will." The command is to be found in the third chapter of *Liber Legis*: "and to each man and woman that thou meetest, were it but to dine or to drink at them, it is the Law to give. Then they shall chance to abide in this bliss or no; it is no odds."

He adapted these versicles to the exigencies for grace before meals; see Letter A for this dialogue. Furthermore, he insisted that each student perform certain exercises and prayers at set times during the day, primarily that the whole pattern of life be thus dedicated to the Great Work. He coined a phrase "background-concentration" for this procedure. It implied that by so doing, a tendency would be initiated toward concentration which would stand the student in good stead when, or as, he approached the problem of teaching the mind to center itself. Letter A gives much of this approach, but the concept is scattered throughout the book.

His signature appended to all the letters is always "666." This may require a few words of explanation for the reader who has not read other Crowley books and become familiar with the symbol.

Crowley was brought up in a household dominated by the religion of the Plymouth Brethren in England. This is a fundamentalist Christian sect which, among many other things, regarded the Bible literally as the inspired word of God. Thus it could not be changed in any way, and had to serve as the basis for general daily behavior throughout life. In this household, he was permitted no other literature to read other than the Bible until he was about twelve years of age. Thus he became steeped in Biblical lore, having read it and studied it throughout the years.

His mother, in moments of exasperation no doubt, would call him a "beast." With his knowledge of the Bible, it did not take him long to find out about the Beast of the Book of Revelation, the Beast who was anti-Christ, the Beast whose number was 666. He ultimately identified himself with that Beast, without question aided and abetted by his mother.

When the time came to revolt and to turn against the religion of his family, with all the venom and brilliance that he, and only he, could muster, there could be no alternative but that he had to ally himself with those forces which were opposed to the stupidities his mother stood for. So he became the Beast. And since Revelation counted the number of the Beast and found it to be 666, the number of a Man, he turned all his Qabalistic and philosophical skill in later years toward finding this number in any meaningful word or motto that came his way. Still later, after he had received Liber Legis and was forced, as it were, to obey its precepts, then it was that he begun to sign all communications with that significant number.

Several of the letters describe a method for studying the Qabalah which deserves more than casual notice. I am calling attention to it specifically for fear that otherwise this approach to it specifically for fear that otherwise this approach may be overlooked in the mass of new ideas which will be hurled at the student if he is approaching this subject for the first time.

The method is one that he started to use shortly after joining the Hermetic Order of the Golden Dawn when taken under the wind of Allan Bennett who had become his guru. Wherever he went, he took special notice of any person, object or event with a view to placing it on the Qabalistic Tree of Life. Slowly, in this way, he became adept in using the Tree as a referent for all phenomena whatsoever, and the so-called stereotyped attributions of color, planet, Tarot card, etc., lost their abstract formality and became living things.

I want to quote one paragraph from letter F where this method is described.

> *As I walked about, I made a point of attributing everything I saw to its appropriate idea. I would walk out of the door of my house and reflect that door is Daleth, and house Beth; now the word dob is Hebrew for bear, and has the number 6, which refers to the Sun. Then you come to the fence of your property and that is Cheth–number 8, number of Tarot Trump 7, which is the Chariot; so you begin to look about for your car. Then you come to the street and the first house you see is number 86, and that is Elohim, and it is build of red brick which reminds you of Mars and the Blasted Tower, and so on. As soon as this sort of work, which can be done in a quite lighthearted spirit, becomes habitual, you will find your mind running naturally in this direction, and will be surprised at your progress. Never let your mind wander from the fact that your Qabalah is not my Qabalah; a good many of the things which I have noted may be useful to you, but you must construct your own system so that it is a living weapon in your hand.*

The novelist Philip Wylie, many years ago earned a reputation for himself by the writing of a book entitled *A Generation of Vipers* in which he excoriated mothers and motherhood. This was one of many books denouncing so-called mother love, laying down the proposition, which has since been enormously elaborated, that this has led to the emasculation of the American male, placing him in emotional servitude to the American matriarchy.

The book created an ever-widening stir, and has left its mark on American literature, or at least the literature of popular psychology. If Freud originally developed the concept of the Oedipus complex at some length, replete with innumerable case histories and paradigms, then Philip Wylie extended it with great power in order to reach the general public.

But the most bitter and violent of all the attacks on mother love that I am familiar with has emanated from Crowley. His letter 53 has to be read slowly and closely to be fully appreciated. It is far more deadly and vitriolic than anything Freud ever wrote, and much more to the point than Wylie's work. No doubt it is predicated on the bad relationship he had with his own mother, of whom he has written at length in *The Confessions of Aleister Crowley* (New York: Hill and Wang, 1970). I have elaborated upon this in a rather different direction and with other details in *The Eye in the Triangle* (St. Paul: Llewellyn Publications, 1970).

Magick without Tears is chock-full of descriptions of unusual things, strange events, weird people and stories which make for fascinating reading. Much of the material, for example, about the history as well as the possible application of *Liber Legis* is so extraordinary as almost to deserve extrapolation to form a small book by itself.

There is one story briefly mentioned in letter 80 which Crowley must have written years earlier, though the manuscript has been lost and I have never seen any reference to it outside of this book. Entitled "Every Precaution," it packs sufficient dramatic wallop to excite some novelist enough to do a short story on it. Other stories are gruesome and macabre to a degree, like that of the woman-cheese-rat-murders toward the end of the volume, which are ghoulish and almost incredible to most of us who lead more prosaic lives.

Anecdotes relative to his wide travels and variegated experiences render this a unique piece of reading material. Finally, his descriptions of Magick and Yoga (seemingly contradictory approaches to self-discovery), their resemblances and differences, are among the most lucid and illuminating, to say nothing of being provocative, that I have ever seen anywhere at any time.

I cannot help but feel that the beginner in these studies as well as the advanced student will discover in these letters a veritable mine of important information and an encyclopedia of occult learning not to be found elsewhere. Though the title of he book may be amusing, the contents are far from being so. Crowley's reputation as a writer and teacher of the greatest magnitude must be enhance by these letters, which are thus strongly recommended to all who seek the Light.

There are some magnificent flashes of profundity in this book as when Crowley examines the necessity of keeping a diary, a personal record of all practices undertaken. A great deal of what we know about him is due to the fact that he kept a diary throughout his life. Most of these are intact and have been preserved, thanks to the scrupulousness and care of Mr. Gerald Yorke, to whom posterity will have much to be thankful for. Only a few sections have been lost due to Crowley's constant moving from pillar to post, and the carelessness of those around him.

Anyway, he offers some meaningful suggestions when he considers the diary in relationship to the magical memory. He is far clearer and more provocative on this subject than he has ever been before. Again, these insights are confined to no one particular letter but are scattered through all of them.

The interested student could keep several notebooks, each devoted to some particular subject, such as the magical memory.

In this way, he could prepare several very interesting notebooks on specific magical topics based on this particular work.

Some reviewers in this country of *The Confessions of Aleister Crowley* have likened him to a Victorian hippy. Because he was unconventional in his sex life, experimented freely with drugs and dressed exotically at times, he has been pictured as the prototype of the modern hippy. There appears at first to be some justification for this identification–provided one does not examine the thesis too closely. But dig deeper and the resemblance falls apart altogether. There is enough data presented in this striking set of letters, apart from anything else the man has written in his long literary life, to thoroughly destroy any such possibility. A bohemian and eccentric he may well have been–a hippy never! Many of the young people of today are turning toward his writing with a view of resolving some of the most serious problems of our time–conflicts which affect them and our society most seriously. In this, I think they are showing some deep wisdom. But in many of their overt attitudes and behavior, it seems as if they are missing the boat entirely. This is why it is imperative that they become familiar with the tenets of these letters, to make them part and parcel of their own mental and spiritual equipment. They may find a variety of answers or suggestions which, if followed, could result in a transformation of their lives and those of succeeding generations.

(1) For sloppiness and untidiness, Crowley had absolutely no use. Only when on expeditions of one kind or another, did he ever look grimy or untidy. Otherwise he was fastidious to a degree, and proud of it. Not that he was compulsive or an exponent of conforming to social dictates or the arbitrary whims of current fashion–far from it. He was violently opposed to such conformist attitudes, a true rebel toward that as to almost everything else.

(2) Like many of today's generation, he used drugs. He had experimented with many psychedelic agents–with some that are totally unfamiliar to our young folk today. Because of Allan

Bennett's asthma, drugs were experimented with to experience relief from the bronchial paroxysms and dyspnoea. And incidental and not anticipated effect at first was the psychedelic effect, the inadvertent experience of mystical states of consciousness. These occurred, I am inclined to believe, not merely because of the pharmacodynamism of the drug but because Allan was mystically inclined, and because he had already undergone considerable magical training in the Hermetic Order of the Golden Dawn.

Whatever knowledge Allan had obtained about pharmacology was passed on to the disciple, Aleister Crowley, when he came under the tutelage of Allan. The result was that, long before he in turn developed asthma, he conducted experiments with a wide variety of drugs in order to determine whether by their means a door could be opened, or held open, to higher mystical states. But Crowley came to insist that these drugs be left severely alone until or unless you knew what you were doing. Experiment, yes–but with care. Again and again, this caution is insisted upon in no uncertain terms in dozens of different writings. In fact, I wish these works on drugs were better known to the contemporary scene, for what he had to say could serve as a guide into the unknown and immeasurable regions of the mind and spirit. For a reprint of his essays about hashish with an acute analysis of mystical states in terms of the Buddhist skandhas, the reader should consult *Roll Away the Stone* (St. Paul: Llewellyn Publications, 1968).

Some of the letters in *Magick without Tears* are particularly pertinent to this theme, where these topics are handled simply and directly and intelligently. For example, in letter 78 entitled "Sore Spots," he makes some priceless contributions to the triad of drugs, sex and religion which no one can afford to leave unread. There are many such references. I was profoundly impressed by this particular letter.

(3) He was no "flower-child" dedicated to peace at any price. Though squeamish in all sorts of ways, he was yet capable

of lashing out, shooting someone, or poking them in the nose. Violence, for him, was as much a part of life as peace and quiet. Modern pacifism would have repelled him altogether. He had made it a rule of life to expose himself to all sorts of dangerous situations in which violence was implicit and in which he revelled. Read "The Smoking Dog," a chapter from *The Book of Lies*, quoted in one of these letters. It clarifies his point of view with force and simplicity. Love and Death are likened to the two hounds of God that pursue man, who must ultimately turn and use them.

"Make love not war" certainly would win his approval. But then he might insist on changing the word "not" and replacing it with "and." *The Book of the Law* serves as his authority here, governing his every attitude and moral authority here, governing his every attitude and moral outlook. It gives vast prominence to love–to love under will. But its third and final chapter makes no attempt to soften the hammer blows of violence. "Now let it be first understood that I am a god of War and of Vengeance. I shall deal hardly with them." This is the message of Ra-Hoor-Khuit, the third of the divinities involved in *Liber Legis*, Nuit and Hadit being the other two. "Mercy let be off; damn them who pity! Kill and torture; spare not; be upon them! Many of the letters contain commentaries and interpretations of some of the more enigmatical parts of that book, and it thus becomes a gold mine of information.

Soon *Liber Legis* will be republished by Llewellyn Publications, together with Crowley's protracted commentary that took years in the writing, under the title *The Law Is for All*. I think it is an urgent necessity at this time. But even in these letters comprising *Magick without Tears*, there are some fine gems of interpretation that should not be missed.

(4) Finally, he was capable of what most present-day hippies are not–self discipline. His entire life is a dynamic testimonial to that fact, demonstrating the practice of the disciplines of meditation and

Magick–often without supervision. They transformed him so that when the great illuminations occurred toward the end of the first decade of this century, he coined a Latin motto which, translated, meant "In my lifetime I have conquered the Universe by the force of Truth." Even then, he was not through with his self-discipline. During World War II, when he was in the steadfastly, spiritual and magical disciplines which he mastered, all as described in extant diaries.

His contempt for the undisciplined mob, lolling around on street corners and curbs, is enough to dissipate any possibility of describing him as a Victorian hippy. On the contrary, the moderns, whether hippies or not, need him tremendously and what he has to offer could possibly redeem them.

The end of his letter 45 is adequate reminder of what he stood for: "to advance–that mean Work. Patient, exhausting, thankless, often bewildering Work. Dear sister, if you would but Work! Work blindly, foolishly, misguidedly, it doesn't matter in the end: Work in itself has absolute virtue." Of course the work that he refers to is spiritual work–meditation, Yoga, Magick, in all phases and varieties. Work, not intellectualization. In the footnote to that same letter, he gives a quick rundown of some of his attitudes and early experiences where work is concerned so that his correspondent might not run away with the idea that he was preaching what he had not practiced.

His occult biography *The Temple of Solomon the King*, serialized throughout all the ten numbers of The Equinox, gives ample evidence of his persistence and fidelity where the Great Work was concerned.

Above all, notice the remarks as the beginning of letter 45. The ideas expressed there are in reality at the heart of his system of training and development. The chiding he administers to his correspondent is not nearly as severe as he had been known to give himself.

Throughout these letters are innumerable references to *The Equinox*. To the younger student of today, *The Equinox* may convey but little until he attempts to purchase one or more of them. He will find it all but impossible. Even if he succeeds in tracking some of them down, he will discover that the tag attached to them bears an exorbitant price. (I have heard only recently a set of the eleven volumes being sold for $500.) For this reason, Llewellyn Publications is republishing selected writings from *The Equinox*, entitled *Gems from The Equinox*, which falls within a price range that is compatible with the pocketbook of most students.

But what are these books? Between 1909 and 1914, Aleister Crowley published in England a large, beautifully printed periodical. The masthead on the cover bore two phrases: "The Aim of Religion" and "The Method of Science." This periodical contained a wide assortment of verse, plays, short stories and miscellaneous occult material. One issue appeared every six months, at the Spring and Autumnal Equinoxes, of that five year period. Ten enormous issues appeared in all.

After 1914 there was a hiatus of five years, corresponding to World War I, when Crowley was domiciled in the U.S. He called it a five year period of silence, which was ultimately broken by the appearance of another large volume bound in blue cloth–called colloquially the Blue Equinox. No others were published; there was no more money available.

By students of occultism, these volumes were regarded as a veritable gold mine of occult lore. Most who bought them were far less interested in the wide literary assortment offered. Yoga and Magick were what these books stood for, and this where *The Equinox* excelled.

There was simply nothing like them elsewhere. In these instructions about the occult arts, Crowley used superb prose, and clarified the subject matter by eliminating all the superstition, dross and fantasy that had been attached to these topics. They were masterpieces of instruction. It was for these reasons that the eleven volumes of *The Equinox* were so zealously sought after throughout the years.

In letter 75, Crowley has written a word or two about what he intended to accomplish in these books. What he has to say is so interesting that the following is quoted from that letter.

> *My special job was to preserve the Sacred Tradition, so that a new Renaissance might in the due season rekindle the hidden Light. I was accordingly to make a Quintessence of the Ancient Wisdom, and publish it in as permanent a form as possible. This I did in* The Equinox. *I should perhaps have been strictly classified, and admitted only the "Publication in Class A," "A-B," "B," and "D" material. But I had the idea that it would be a good plan to add all sorts of other stuff, so that people who were not in any way interested in the real Work might preserve their copies... "They" [the Secret Chiefs of the Order]...were agreed on measures calculated to assure the survival of the Wisdom worth saving until the time, perhaps three hundred or six hundred year later, when a new current should revive the shattered thought of mankind.* The Equinox, *in a word, was to be a sort of Rosetta Stone.*

It appears that he recognized that he should have published only the basic yoga and magical instructions known as the Official Instructions of the Order in order to preserve "the Sacred Tradition." Now that the original sets of *The Equinox* are out of circulation–there were only one thousand sets printed–it seems necessary to reissue the fundamental material that he had in mind at the beginning–the official instructions. Thus *Gems from the Equinox* consists solely of those. If it was the wish of the so-called Secret Chiefs of the Order to preserve the practical Wisdom of the hidden Sanctuaries against the disasters of war, natural cataclysms and famine–all of which now seem clearly in the offing–I hope that the issuance of *Gems from The Equinox* will assist in the fulfillment of the original intent, freed from the addition "of all sorts of other stuff." For thus freed, this set of reprints of the Official Publications of the A∴A∴ now coincides with what appears to have been Crowley's original intent as expressed in *Magick without Tears*.

Magick without Tears demanded that some careful pruning be done. I have exercised great caution and deliberation in the editing, if only because I am fully aware of the fanatical attitude of some Crowley disciples. Every word that he wrote must have been endowed with some divine quality and must not be tampered with–so runs their belief. It is quite irrational. Crowley himself would have been the first to admit this, though he has often admitted that he was altogether incapable of editing his own material. The only thing ever to issue from his pen which he demanded must never be edited was a group of select writings called *The Holy Books*, and above all, *The Book of the Law*. "Change not so much as the style of a letter...."

What I have deleted is mostly rambling or repetitious statements, a few quotations from Robert Browning–none of which in any case interfere with the meaning of any particular passage. This is then the cardinal rule that has applied at all times during the surgical intervention to the text of these letters. Nothing has been changed that might alter his free flow of ideas or the intrinsic meaning of the communication. Thus the bulk of the volume has been reduced, but it has been tightened up considerably, thus making for easier reading. There were a few letters so complete and firmly written that no editing was required in the least.

Stray bits of revealing insight without parallel elsewhere shine here and there. For example, he is almost at his best in letter

20 on the significance of Lamens and Talismans and Pantacles. It is worth comparing his clarity here with some earlier elucidations, notably the delightful Part II of *Book 4* or in *Magick in Theory and Practice*. Invariably it turns out that no real comparison can be made, though in these letters there is a maturity and clarify that is not found in either of the books just mentioned.

Again, when he discusses Gods and Angels, he is so direct and matter of fact as to be altogether impressive. He makes no attempt to be sanctimonious, other-worldly or guru-like, but deals with abstruse problems easily, without being afraid to say occasionally "I don't know." One is impressed by his honesty and forthrightness. There is no other writer on this subject today who can hold a candle to him.

Another matter touched upon in these letters is a phenomenon that is current today. Groups of young people are breaking away from the mainstream of society or the so-called establishment, to form little communes which they hope will be free from the disease which they see attacking society. They want none of it. They have high ideals, believing it possible to form utopias of one kind or another where corruption, hypocrisy and deceit will be unable to flourish. There are hundreds of such communes all over the country–all searching for a utopia.

"I have no patience whatever with Utopia-mongers," wrote Crowley.

> *Biology simply shouts at us that the happy contented community, everyone with his own (often highly specialized) job, nobody in need, nobody in danger, is necessarily stagnant. Termites and other ants, bees, beavers; these and many another have produced perfect systems. What is the first characteristic? Stupidity. "Where there is no vision, the people shall perish." What is the Fighter Termite to*

do, after he has been blocked out of his home? None of these communities possess any resource at all against any unforeseen unfavorable change of circumstances.... Nor does anyone of them show any achievement; having got to the end of their biological tether, they stay put, without an aim, an idea, an effort.

If the utopian community or ideal is unworkable, what then are the conditions of progress? "Number One is obviously Irregularity, Eccentricity, Disorder, the Revolutionary Spirit, Experiment."

These are obviously characteristics of Crowley himself as a person, and so we should expect him to project these as being the prerequisites for progress.

His description of the so-called "crazy" adventurer who embodies these characteristics, or the holy man, should also be read in conjunction with that lengthy section of *The Book of Thoth* which describes in great detail the several interpretations of the Tarot card "The Fool." It may facilitate also some understanding of how he finally came to conceive of himself. On several occasions he has essayed this task, not only in this fascinating book of letters, and in the book about the Tarot, but in his earlier book *Magick in Theory and Practice*. It is far from easy for the ordinary individual, bound by the ordinary codes of social behavior and the conventional frames of reference, to have the foggiest idea of what moves or motivates an initiate whose illumination has imposed an entirely new point of view on the world and life in general. The whole of letter 79 on "Progress" should be read in this connection.

It is also interesting to compare some of the weird historical facts quoted in letter 48 and other regarding Adolf Hitler, Soror I.W.E., and *The Book of the Law*, with some of the fairy stories and fantasies spun in a relatively recent book entitled *The Dawn of Magic* (some editions have entitled it *The Morning of the Magicians*) by Louis Pauwels and Jacques Bergier. I have to admit that some of the material relative to the history of the Golden Dawn is so far out, so historically false, as to make one doubt the veracity of other ideas with which one may be less familiar. It thus makes one doubt the validity of what the authors state about the Hitler theme, and several others. However, some of the references in *Magick without Tears* to Hitler and Soror I.W.E.'s foolish attempts to get Hitler to adopt *Liber Legis* as his personal code to foist upon Germany and then mankind are enough to make one pause.

In conclusion, I should add that the Foreword to this book was written by Karl Germer. He was Crowley's representative in America and his successor as Outer Head of the Ordo Templi Orientis. The Foreword describes in part how this collection of letters came into being. Aleister Crowley wrote the Introduction, which consists of several preliminary letters, paving the way for the remaining ones. I have written the Preface to highlight some of the more outstanding contents of the book which ought not to be missed.

Did any book ever have so many messengers as this one? I hope they will not be confusing to the reader, but that all of them will somehow conduce to his further and deeper understanding.

                                                            Israel Regardie
                                                            June 6, 1970
                                                           Studio City, Calif.

The Alchemist's Handbook
By Frater Albertus
Copyright 1974 Paracelsus Research Society

FOREWORD
By Israel Regardie

This is the age of "how to do" books. There is one on almost any subject you can think of. Since they fill a variety of needs, they have proven a boon. From them you can learn to paint, sew, plant a herb garden, build a brick barbecue in the backyard, become an interior decorator, and re-wire your own home. Almost every imaginable topic has been covered by these books. So if you assumed that this Manual falls in this category, you would be right–save for the simple fact that it is a great deal more.

Alchemy has exerted a strange fascination over mankind for centuries. The underlying philosophical theorum was that if the Divine Will had originally acted upon the *prima materia* to produce the precious metals and all else, why should not the alchemist–purified in mind and body, and an expert in the then known laboratory techniques–seek to emulate the same natural process in a shorter span of time? One has only to read a good history of chemistry, or to peruse a little of the vast alchemical literature, to become aware of its awful seductiveness. Men have left homes and families, squandered fortunes, incurred sickness and disease, gambled away prestige, social and other positions in quest of the goals perceived in the alchemical dream–longevity, perfect health, and the ability to transmute base metals into gold.

One must not be deluded by superficialities here. The alchemical adepts were patently dedicated and God-fearing men, holding the highest spiritual ideals conceivable. It is too bad more practitioners of the art did not perceive these goals.

Only recently, a journalist wrote that the Paracelsus Research Society which sponsors this Manual, offered to teach alchemy in two *weeks*. How could one be so myopic? Or illiterate?

In the early fourteenth century, Bonus of Ferrara spoke of Alchemy as "the key of all good things, the Art of Art, the Science of Sciences." Not only was the alchemist to be concerned with the purification of metal and the elimination of sickness and disease from the human race, but he affirmed that Alchemy as Science and Art provided both a means to synthesize all the other sciences and a training of the intellectual and spiritual faculties.

The fascination that Alchemy has always held over mankind has surely been tainted in that rarely were there higher institutions of learning where the proper techniques and methods might be learned as with other arts and sciences. No doubt, after the manner of the mysterious seventeenth century Rosicrucians, individual disciples were selected and trained by a master alchemist. We know that they had assistants and apprentices–for who would have kept the fires stoked in the furnaces, and washed the unending stream of glass and clay utensils employed in calcining, separating and distilling? Or who would have done all the thousand and one menial things that are so easily performed today that we barely have to think about them? But whether or not these assistants were ever encouraged to learn or to acquire the requisite disciplines and procedures–this is problematical.

In the vast literature on the subject, there is nothing that I have ever found that even pretended to demonstrate fundamental principles. Traditional alchemy, with its emphasis on piety, secrecy and allegory, is admittedly obscure. Over the years, I have met many men who could talk a good line about alchemy, but nothing practical ever emerged from them. Nor did anyone volunteer to demonstrate its basic truths in a laboratory or over the kitchen stove. Not one–until I met the author of this Manual some years ago. Not one–until I read the first limited edition of this Manual which literally is worth its weight in gold.

Incidentally, a few years ago I wrote something in recommendation of this manual, yet expressing criticism of its literary style, its form of expression, the innumerable typographical errors. This was silly and arrogant. For even if, theoretically, the book were written in the worst possible style, it would still be unique and a genuine masterpiece. Had it not been written and published, we would be the losers by far. It teaches with clarity, simplicity and accuracy the technical means whereby the lesser circulation may be accomplished. It should be a revelation to those who have not previously been introduced to this method of dealing with herbs. The Great Work is said to be essentially an extension of the same process, the same techniques, with the same universal philosophy. Many an alchemist of former years would have given his eyeteeth–or surely a small fortune–for this information. Many might have been spared disaster and destruction had they been familiar with the data contained in this Manual.

Descriptions of the alchemical processes are not readily understood in terms of modern chemistry. This is not to say that some formal training in high school or first-year college chemistry would not be useful. At the very least, it would have provided the dexterity to use the equipment also used in alchemy. But even if it were possible to translate the one system into the terminology of the other, the alchemists are haunted by the fear of revealing too much, too easily, or too soon–thus opening the way to abuse. Modern man has shown himself to be an adept in the art of abusing nature, as all our current emphasis on ecology and environmental pollution has indicated. So there is considerable justification for their doubts and for the allegorical mode of expression they have deliberately chosen.

But do not be deceived. Simply as this book is written, alchemy is a hard taskmaster. It demands patient and laborious service. There is no simple or easy path to the Great Work. It requires great dedication of purpose, sincerity and willingness to pursue this path to the bitter end–no matter at what cost.

One of the older alchemists stated that the fundamental process is so simple that even women and children could accomplish it. Maybe! It is only after one has arrived at the other shore, as it were, that one can realize that "except ye become as little children ye cannot enter the kingdom of heaven." Meanwhile, it requires effort, labor and prayer–or its equivalents–to achieve the simple child–like state capable of achieving the goals of alchemy. Not many have been blessed with the special genetic or psychological structure, or the perseverance, or the grace of God to find it.

But, if you really want to learn the basic principles of practical alchemy, here they are in this wonderful little Manual. There is no other book that I have ever encountered in all my long years in this movement that is one fraction as clear or as helpful. Forty years in this movement that is one fraction as clear or as helpful. Forty years ago, I would have found it far more intriguing and illuminating than Mrs. Atwood's heavy and ponderous tome on which I exercised my wisdom teeth. Study it–and work at the processes described. Practice is so much more rewarding and enlightening than a sterile "head-trip." *Ora et labore*. Pry and work–*but work*. Without this you cannot even begin. And this book describes *how* to go to work, and with what.

Israel Regardie

New Falcon Publications
Publisher of Controversial Books and CDs
Invites You to Visit Our Website:
http://www.newfalcon.com

At the Falcon website you can:

- Browse the online catalog of all our great titles, including books by Robert Anton Wilson, Christopher S. Hyatt, Israel Regardie, Aleister Crowley, Timothy Leary, Osho, Lon Milo DuQuette and many more
- Find out what's available and what's out of stock
- Get special discounts
- Order our titles through our secure online server
- Find products not available anywhere else including:
    - One of a kind and limited availability products
    - Special packages
    - Special pricing
- And much, much more

Get online today at http://www.newfalcon.com